Jessamyn West, MLib
Editor

Digital versus Non-Digital Reference: Ask a Librarian Online and Offline

Digital versus Non-Digital Reference: Ask a Librarian Online and Offline has been co-published simultaneously as *The Reference Librarian*, Number 85 2004.

Pre-publication
REVIEWS,
COMMENTARIES,
EVALUATIONS . . .

"USEFUL FOR LIBRARIES CONSIDER-ING CHAT REFERENCE SERVICE. Public, law, and academic libraries are represented, as are archives and commercial services. The chapter on planning multilingual chat reference service will be useful for libraries with diverse populations."

Jenny Tobias, MLS
Librarian
Collection Development
Museum of Modern Art
New York City

The Haworth Information Press
An Imprint of The Haworth Press, Inc.

Digital versus Non-Digital Reference:
Ask a Librarian
Online and Offline

Digital versus Non-Digital Reference: Ask a Librarian Online and Offline has been co-published simultaneously as *The Reference Librarian*, Number 85 2004.

The Reference Librarian Monographic "Separates"

Below is a list of "separates," which in serials librarianship means a special issue simultaneously published as a special journal issue or double-issue *and* as a "separate" hardbound monograph. (This is a format which we also call a "DocuSerial.")

"Separates" are published because specialized libraries or professionals may wish to purchase a specific thematic issue by itself in a format which can be separately cataloged and shelved, as opposed to purchasing the journal on an on-going basis. Faculty members may also more easily consider a "separate" for classroom adoption.

"Separates" are carefully classified separately with the major book jobbers so that the journal tie-in can be noted on new book order slips to avoid duplicate purchasing.

You may wish to visit Haworth's Website at . . .

http://www.HaworthPress.com

. . . to search our online catalog for complete tables of contents of these separates and related publications.

You may also call 1-800-HAWORTH (outside US/Canada: 607-722-5857), or Fax 1-800-895-0582 (outside US/Canada: 607-771-0012), or e-mail at:

docdelivery@haworthpress.com

Digital versus Non-Digital Reference: Ask a Librarian Online and Offline, edited by Jessamyn West, MLib (No. 85, 2004). *A librarian's guide to commercial Ask A Librarian (AskA) and tutorial services and how they compare to traditional library services.*

Cooperative Reference: Social Interaction in the Workplace, edited by Celia Hales Mabry, PhD (No. 83/84, 2003). *This informative volume focuses on effective social interactions between library co-workers, presenting perspectives, firsthand accounts, and advice from experienced and successful reference librarians.*

Outreach Services in Academic and Special Libraries, edited by Paul Kelsey, MLIS, and Sigrid Kelsey, MLIS (No. 82, 2003). *Presents an array of models and case studies for creating and implementing outreach services in academic and special library settings.*

Managing the Twenty-First Century Reference Department: Challenges and Prospects, edited by Kwasi Sarkodie-Mensah, PhD (No. 81, 2003). *An up-to-date guide on managing and maintaining a reference department in the twenty-first century.*

Digital Reference Services, edited by Bill Katz, PhD (No. 79/80, 2002/2003). *A clear and concise book explaining developments in electronic technology for reference services and their implications for reference librarians.*

The Image and Role of the Librarian, edited by Wendi Arant, MLS, and Candace R. Benefiel, MA, MLIS (No. 78, 2002). *A unique and insightful examination of how librarians are perceived–and how they perceive themselves.*

Distance Learning: Information Access and Services for Virtual Users, edited by Hemalata Iyer, PhD (No. 77, 2002). *Addresses the challenge of providing Web-based library instructional materials in a time of ever-changing technologies.*

Helping the Difficult Library Patron: New Approaches to Examining and Resolving a Long-Standing and Ongoing Problem, edited by Kwasi Sarkodie-Mensah, PhD (No. 75/76, 2002). *"Finally! A book that fills in the information cracks not covered in library school about the ubiquitous problem patron. Required reading for public service librarians." (Cheryl LaGuardia, MLS, Head of Instructional Services for the Harvard College Library, Cambridge, Massachusetts)*

Evolution in Reference and Information Services: The Impact of the Internet, edited by Di Su, MLS (No. 74, 2001). *Helps you make the most of the changes brought to the profession by the Internet.*

Doing the Work of Reference: Practical Tips for Excelling as a Reference Librarian, edited by Celia Hales Mabry, PhD (No. 72 and 73, 2001). *"An excellent handbook for reference librarians who wish to move from novice to expert. Topical coverage is extensive and is presented by the best guides possible: practicing reference librarians." (Rebecca Watson-Boone, PhD, President, Center for the Study of Information Professionals, Inc.)*

New Technologies and Reference Services, edited by Bill Katz, PhD (No. 71, 2000). *This important book explores developing trends in publishing, information literacy in the reference environment, reference provision in adult basic and community education, searching sessions, outreach programs, locating moving image materials for multimedia development, and much more.*

Reference Services for the Adult Learner: Challenging Issues for the Traditional and Technological Era, edited by Kwasi Sarkodie-Mensah, PhD (No. 69/70, 2000). *Containing research from librarians and adult learners from the United States, Canada, and Australia, this comprehensive guide offers you strategies for teaching adult patrons that will enable them to properly use and easily locate all of the materials in your library.*

Library Outreach, Partnerships, and Distance Education: Reference Librarians at the Gateway, edited by Wendi Arant and Pixey Anne Mosley (No. 67/68, 1999). *Focuses on community outreach in libraries toward a broader public by extending services based on recent developments in information technology.*

From Past-Present to Future-Perfect: A Tribute to Charles A. Bunge and the Challenges of Contemporary Reference Service, edited by Chris D. Ferguson, PhD (No. 66, 1999). *Explore reprints of selected articles by Charles Bunge, bibliographies of his published work, and original articles that draw on Bunge's values and ideas in assessing the present and shaping the future of reference service.*

Reference Services and Media, edited by Martha Merrill, PhD (No. 65, 1999). *Gives you valuable information about various aspects of reference services and media, including changes, planning issues, and the use and impact of new technologies.*

Coming of Age in Reference Services: A Case History of the Washington State University Libraries, edited by Christy Zlatos, MSLS (No. 64, 1999). *A celebration of the perseverance, ingenuity, and talent of the librarians who have served, past and present, at the Holland Library reference desk.*

Document Delivery Services: Contrasting Views, edited by Robin Kinder, MLS (No. 63, 1999). *Reviews the planning and process of implementing document delivery in four university libraries–Miami University, University of Colorado at Denver, University of Montana at Missoula, and Purdue University Libraries.*

The Holocaust: Memories, Research, Reference, edited by Robert Hauptman, PhD, and Susan Hubbs Motin (No. 61/62, 1998). *"A wonderful resource for reference librarians, students, and teachers . . . on how to present this painful, historical event." (Ephraim Kaye, PhD, The International School for Holocaust Studies, Yad Vashem, Jerusalem)*

Electronic Resources: Use and User Behavior, edited by Hemalata Iyer, PhD (No. 60, 1998). *Covers electronic resources and their use in libraries, with emphasis on the Internet and the Geographic Information Systems (GIS).*

Philosophies of Reference Service, edited by Celia Hales Mabry (No. 59, 1997). *"Recommended reading for any manager responsible for managing reference services and hiring reference librarians in any type of library." (Charles R. Anderson, MLS, Associate Director for Public Services, King County Library System, Bellevue, Washington)*

Business Reference Services and Sources: How End Users and Librarians Work Together, edited by Katherine M. Shelfer (No. 58, 1997). *"This is an important collection of papers suitable for all business librarians. . . . Highly recommended!" (Lucy Heckman, MLS, MBA, Business and Economics Reference Librarian, St. John's University, Jamaica, New York)*

Reference Sources on the Internet: Off the Shelf and onto the Web, edited by Karen R. Diaz (No. 57, 1997). *Surf off the library shelves and onto the Internet and cut your research time in half!*

Reference Services for Archives and Manuscripts, edited by Laura B. Cohen (No. 56, 1997). *"Features stimulating and interesting essays on security in archives, ethics in the archival profession, and electronic records." ("The Year's Best Professional Reading" (1998), Library Journal)*

Career Planning and Job Searching in the Information Age, edited by Elizabeth A. Lorenzen, MLS (No. 55, 1996). *"Offers stimulating background for dealing with the issues of technology and service. . . . A reference tool to be looked at often." (The One-Person Library)*

The Roles of Reference Librarians: Today and Tomorrow, edited by Kathleen Low, MLS (No. 54, 1996). *"A great asset to all reference collections. . . . Presents important, valuable information for reference librarians as well as other library users." (Library Times International)*

Reference Services for the Unserved, edited by Fay Zipkowitz, MSLS, DA (No. 53, 1996). *"A useful tool in developing strategies to provide services to all patrons." (Science Books & Films)*

Library Instruction Revisited: Bibliographic Instruction Comes of Age, edited by Lyn Elizabeth M. Martin, MLS (No. 51/52, 1995). *"A powerful collection authored by respected practitioners who have stormed the bibliographic instruction (BI) trenches and, luckily for us, have recounted their successes and shortcomings." (The Journal of Academic Librarianship)*

Library Users and Reference Services, edited by Jo Bell Whitlatch, PhD (No. 49/50, 1995). *"Well-planned, balanced, and informative. . . . Both new and seasoned professionals will find material for service attitude formation and practical advice for the front lines of service." (Anna M. Donnelly, MS, MA, Associate Professor and Reference Librarian, St. John's University Library)*

Social Science Reference Services, edited by Pam Baxter, MLS (No. 48, 1995). *"Offers practical guidance to the reference librarian. . . . A valuable source of information about specific literatures within the social sciences and the skills and techniques needed to provide access to those literatures." (Nancy P. O'Brien, MLS, Head, Education and Social Science Library, and Professor of Library Administration, University of Illinois at Urbana-Champaign)*

Reference Services in the Humanities, edited by Judy Reynolds, MLS (No. 47, 1994). *"A well-chosen collection of situations and challenges encountered by reference librarians in the humanities." (College Research Library News)*

Racial and Ethnic Diversity in Academic Libraries: Multicultural Issues, edited by Deborah A. Curry, MLS, MA, Susan Griswold Blandy, MEd, and Lyn Elizabeth M. Martin, MLS (No. 45/46, 1994). *"The useful techniques and attractive strategies presented here will provide the incentive for fellow professionals in academic libraries around the country to go and do likewise in their own institutions." (David Cohen, Adjunct Professor of Library Science, School of Library and Information Science, Queens College; Director, EMIE (Ethnic Materials Information Exchange); Editor, EMIE Bulletin)*

School Library Reference Services in the 90s: Where We Are, Where We're Heading, edited by Carol Truett, PhD (No. 44, 1994). *"Unique and valuable to the the teacher-librarian as well as students of librarianship. . . . The overall work successfully interweaves the concept of the continuously changing role of the teacher-librarian." (Emergency Librarian)*

Reference Services Planning in the 90s, edited by Gail Z. Eckwright, MLS, and Lori M. Keenan, MLS (No. 43, 1994). *"This monograph is well-researched and definitive, encompassing reference service as practices by library and information scientists. . . . It should be required reading for all professional librarian trainees." (Feliciter)*

Librarians on the Internet: Impact on Reference Services, edited by Robin Kinder, MLS (No. 41/42, 1994). *"Succeeds in demonstrating that the Internet is becoming increasingly a challenging but practical and manageable tool in the reference librarian's ever-expanding armory." (Reference Reviews)*

Reference Service Expertise, edited by Bill Katz (No. 40, 1993). *This important volume presents a wealth of practical ideas for improving the art of reference librarianship.*

Modern Library Technology and Reference Services, edited by Samuel T. Huang, MLS, MS (No. 39, 1993). *"This book packs a surprising amount of information into a relatively few number of pages. . . . This book will answer many questions." (Science Books and Films)*

Assessment and Accountability in Reference Work, edited by Susan Griswold Blandy, Lyn M. Martin, and Mary L. Strife (No. 38, 1992). *"An important collection of well-written, real-world chapters addressing the central questions that surround performance and services in all libraries." (Library Times International)*

The Reference Librarian and Implications of Mediation, edited by M. Keith Ewing, MLS, and Robert Hauptman, MLS (No. 37, 1992). *"An excellent and thorough analysis of reference mediation. . . . Well worth reading by anyone involved in the delivery of reference services." (Fred Batt, MLS, Associate University Librarian for Public Services, California State University, Sacramento)*

Library Services for Career Planning, Job Searching and Employment Opportunities, edited by Byron Anderson, MA, MLS (No. 36, 1992). *"An interesting book which tells professional libraries how to set up career information centers. . . . Clearly valuable reading for anyone establishing a career library." (Career Opportunities News)*

In the Spirit of 1992: Access to Western European Libraries and Literature, edited by Mary M. Huston, PhD, and Maureen Pastine, MLS (No. 35, 1992). *"A valuable and practical [collection] which every subject specialist in the field would do well to consult." (Western European Specialists Section Newsletter)*

Access Services: The Convergence of Reference and Technical Services, edited by Gillian M. McCombs, ALA (No. 34, 1992). *"Deserves a wide readership among both technical and public services librarians. . . . Highly recommended for any librarian interested in how reference and technical services roles may be combined." (Library Resources & Technical Services)*

Opportunities for Reference Services: The Bright Side of Reference Services in the 1990s, edited by Bill Katz (No. 33, 1991). *"A well-deserved look at the brighter side of reference services. . . . Should be read by reference librarians and their administrators in all types of libraries." (Library Times International)*

Government Documents and Reference Services, edited by Robin Kinder, MLS (No. 32, 1991). *Discusses access possibilities and policies with regard to government information, covering such important topics as new and impending legislation, information on most frequently used and requested sources, and grant writing.*

The Reference Library User: Problems and Solutions, edited by Bill Katz (No. 31, 1991). *"Valuable information and tangible suggestions that will help us as a profession look critically at our users and decide how they are best served." (Information Technology and Libraries)*

Continuing Education of Reference Librarians, edited by Bill Katz (No. 30/31, 1990). *"Has something for everyone interested in this field. . . . Library trainers and library school teachers may well find stimulus in some of the programs outlined here." (Library Association Record)*

Weeding and Maintenance of Reference Collections, edited by Sydney J. Pierce, PhD, MLS (No. 29, 1990). *"This volume may spur you on to planned activity before lack of space dictates 'ad hoc' solutions." (New Library World)*

Serials and Reference Services, edited by Robin Kinder, MLS, and Bill Katz (No. 27/28, 1990). *"The concerns and problems discussed are those of serials and reference librarians everywhere. . . . The writing is of a high standard and the book is useful and entertaining. . . . This book can be recommended." (Library Association Record)*

Rothstein on Reference: . . . with some help from friends, edited by Bill Katz and Charles Bunge, PhD, MLS (No. 25/26, 1990). *"An important and stimulating collection of essays on reference librarianship. . . . Highly recommended!" (Richard W. Grefrath, MA, MLS, Reference Librarian, University of Nevada Library)* Dedicated to the work of Sam Rothstein, one of the world's most respected teachers of reference librarians, this special volume features his writings as well as articles written about him and his teachings by other professionals in the field.

Integrating Library Use Skills Into the General Education Curriculum, edited by Maureen Pastine, MLS, and Bill Katz (No. 24, 1989). *"All contributions are written and presented to a high standard with excellent references at the end of each. . . . One of the best summaries I have seen on this topic." (Australian Library Review)*

Expert Systems in Reference Services, edited by Christine Roysdon, MLS, and Howard D. White, PhD, MLS (No. 23, 1989). *"The single most comprehensive work on the subject of expert systems in reference service." (Information Processing and Management)*

Information Brokers and Reference Services, edited by Bill Katz and Robin Kinder, MLS (No. 22, 1989). *"An excellent tool for reference librarians and indispensable for anyone seriously considering their own information-brokering service." (Booklist)*

Information and Referral in Reference Services, edited by Marcia Stucklen Middleton, MLS, and Bill Katz (No. 21, 1988). *Investigates a wide variety of situations and models which fall under the umbrella of information and referral.*

Reference Services and Public Policy, edited by Richard Irving, MLS, and Bill Katz (No. 20, 1988). *Looks at the relationship between public policy and information and reports ways in which libraries respond to the need for public policy information.*

Finance, Budget, and Management for Reference Services, edited by Ruth A. Fraley, MLS, MBA, and Bill Katz (No. 19, 1989). *"Interesting and relevant to the current state of financial needs in reference service. . . . A must for anyone new to or already working in the reference service area." (Riverina Library Review)*

Current Trends in Information: Research and Theory, edited by Bill Katz and Robin Kinder, MLS (No. 18, 1987). *"Practical direction to improve reference services and does so in a variety of ways ranging from humorous and clever metaphoric comparisons to systematic and practical methodological descriptions." (American Reference Books Annual)*

International Aspects of Reference and Information Services, edited by Bill Katz and Ruth A. Fraley, MLS, MBA (No. 17, 1987). *"An informative collection of essays written by eminent librarians, library school staff, and others concerned with the international aspects of information work." (Library Association Record)*

Reference Services Today: From Interview to Burnout, edited by Bill Katz and Ruth A. Fraley, MLS, MBA (No. 16, 1987). *Authorities present important advice to all reference librarians on the improvement of service and the enhancement of the public image of reference services.*

The Publishing and Review of Reference Sources, edited by Bill Katz and Robin Kinder, MLS (No. 15, 1987). *"A good review of current reference reviewing and publishing trends in the United States . . . will be of interest to intending reviewers, reference librarians, and students." (Australasian College Libraries)*

Personnel Issues in Reference Services, edited by Bill Katz and Ruth Fraley, MLS, MBA (No. 14, 1986). *"Chock-full of information that can be applied to most reference settings. Recommended for libraries with active reference departments." (RQ)*

Reference Services in Archives, edited by Lucille Whalen (No. 13, 1986). *"Valuable for the insights it provides on the reference process in archives and as a source of information on the different ways of carrying out that process." (Library and Information Science Annual)*

Conflicts in Reference Services, edited by Bill Katz and Ruth A. Fraley, MLS, MBA (No. 12, 1985). *This collection examines issues pertinent to the reference department.*

Evaluation of Reference Services, edited by Bill Katz and Ruth A. Fraley, MLS, MBA (No. 11, 1985). *"A much-needed overview of the present state of the art vis-à-vis reference service evaluation. . . . Excellent. . . . Will appeal to reference professionals and aspiring students." (RQ)*

Library Instruction and Reference Services, edited by Bill Katz and Ruth A. Fraley, MLS, MBA (No. 10, 1984). *"Well written, clear, and exciting to read. This is an important work recommended for all librarians, particularly those involved in, interested in, or considering bibliographic instruction. . . . A milestone in library literature." (RQ)*

Reference Services and Technical Services: Interactions in Library Practice, edited by Gordon Stevenson and Sally Stevenson (No. 9, 1984). *"New ideas and longstanding problems are handled with humor and sensitivity as practical suggestions and new perspectives are suggested by the authors." (Information Retrieval & Library Automation)*

Reference Services for Children and Young Adults, edited by Bill Katz and Ruth A. Fraley, MLS, MBA (No. 7/8, 1983). *"Offers a well-balanced approach to reference service for children and young adults." (RQ)*

Video to Online: Reference Services in the New Technology, edited by Bill Katz and Ruth A. Fraley, MLS, MBA (No. 5/6, 1983). *"A good reference manual to have on hand. . . . Well-written, concise, provide[s] a wealth of information." (Online)*

Ethics and Reference Services, edited by Bill Katz and Ruth A. Fraley, MLS, MBA (No. 4, 1982). *Library experts discuss the major ethical and legal implications that reference librarians must take into consideration when handling sensitive inquiries about confidential material.*

Reference Services Administration and Management, edited by Bill Katz and Ruth A. Fraley, MLS, MBA (No. 3, 1982). *Librarianship experts discuss the management of the reference function in libraries and information centers, outlining the responsibilities and qualifications of reference heads.*

Reference Services in the 1980s, edited by Bill Katz (No. 1/2, 1982). *Here is a thought-provoking volume on the future of reference services in libraries, with an emphasis on the challenges and needs that have come about as a result of automation.*

Digital versus Non-Digital Reference:
Ask a Librarian
Online and Offline

Jessamyn West, MLib
Editor

Digital versus Non-Digital Reference: Ask a Librarian Online and Offline has been co-published simultaneously as *The Reference Librarian*, Number 85 2004.

The Haworth Information Press®
An Imprint of The Haworth Press, Inc.

New York • London • Victoria (AU)
www.HaworthPress.com

Published by

The Haworth Information Press®, 10 Alice Street, Binghamton, NY 13904-1580 USA

The Haworth Information Press® is an imprint of The Haworth Press, Inc., 10 Alice Street, Binghamton, NY 13904-1580 USA.

Digital versus Non-Digital Reference: Ask a Librarian Online and Offline has been co-published simultaneously as *The Reference Librarian*™, Number 85 2004.

Cover design by Lora Wiggins.

Library of Congress Cataloging-in-Publication Data

Digital versus non-digital reference : ask a librarian online and offline / Jessamyn West, editor.
    p. cm.
    "Co-published simultaneoulsy as The reference librarian, number 85, 2004."
    Includes bibliographical references and index.
    ISBN 0-7890-2442-X (hard cover : alk. paper) – ISBN 0-7890-2443-8 (soft cover : alk. paper)
    1. Electronic reference services (Libraries) 2. Reference services (Libraries)–Information technology. 3. Internet in library reference services. 4. Reference services (Libraries) I. West, Jessamyn, 1968- II. Reference librarian.
  Z711.45 .D548 2004
  025.5'2–dc22
                                                2004006246

Indexing, Abstracting & Website/Internet Coverage

The Reference Librarian

This section provides you with a list of major indexing & abstracting services. That is to say, each service began covering this periodical during the year noted in the right column. Most Websites which are listed below have indicated that they will either post, disseminate, compile, archive, cite or alert their own Website users with research-based content from this work. (This list is as current as the copyright date of this publication.)

(continued)

*Exact start date to come.

(continued)

Special bibliographic notes related to special journal issues
(separates) and indexing/abstracting:

- indexing/abstracting services in this list will also cover material in any "separate" that is co-published simultaneously with Haworth's special thematic journal issue or DocuSerial. Indexing/abstracting usually covers material at the article/chapter level.
- monographic co-editions are intended for either non-subscribers or libraries which intend to purchase a second copy for their circulating collections.
- monographic co-editions are reported to all jobbers/wholesalers/approval plans. The source journal is listed as the "series" to assist the prevention of duplicate purchasing in the same manner utilized for books-in-series.
- to facilitate user/access services all indexing/abstracting services are encouraged to utilize the co-indexing entry note indicated at the bottom of the first page of each article/chapter/contribution.
- this is intended to assist a library user of any reference tool (whether print, electronic, online, or CD-ROM) to locate the monographic version if the library has purchased this version but not a subscription to the source journal.
- individual articles/chapters in any Haworth publication are also available through the Haworth Document Delivery Service (HDDS).

Digital versus Non-Digital Reference: Ask a Librarian Online and Offline

CONTENTS

ABOUT THE EDITOR

Jessamyn West, MLib, received a Master's in Librarianship at what is now the University of Washington iSchool. She is a freelance librarian and frequent writer, lecturer, and activist on library issues, specifically the USA PATRIOT Act and the new face of digital reference. She is a member of the American Library Association where she serves as an ALA Councilor. Her first book, *Revolting Librarians Redux*, which she co-edited with Katia Roberto, was published by McFarland in the Spring of 2003. She has been annotating library issues online since 1999 via her website <librarian.net>.

Preface

We've been here before. All librarians know this. Being an information provider or an information conduit means continually adapting to the changing face of information, as well as learning to employ appropriate assessment, technologies, and methods when providing this information to the public. Librarians are, and always have been, astute code switchers, polyglots of information's many languages, translating between reference sources and patrons. Digital reference is one more language we are all attaining fluency in.

When I was in library school and we were learning about the history and future of the Internet, my class read an article about telephony and how it was feared that it would erode the social fabric, and possibly even spread disease. While we chuckle at such handwringing nowadays we see the same sort of back-and-forth quibbles and concerns about using the Internet as not only a reference tool but a reference medium. While most libraries find digital reference inevitable to some degree, the degree of implementation varies widely and, like any other innovation in the U.S. today, vendors are jumping on the bandwagon willy-nilly, offering solutions before problems have even been identified.

Most of my reference desk experience predates digital reference, but I did have the chance to work for an odd competing product, Google Answers. They answer questions using a web interface, for a fee. I was hoping to flex my reference skills and maybe make a few bucks. Instead, my experiences confirmed what I had always suspected: just because you answer questions doesn't make you a library. This Google subdivision is run by a few staffers, who I never met or even knew by name, and several hundred contractors, called "Researchers," with vary-

[Haworth co-indexing entry note]: "Preface." West, Jessamyn. Co-published simultaneously in *The Reference Librarian* (The Haworth Information Press, an imprint of The Haworth Press, Inc.) No. 85, 2004, pp. xix-xx; and: *Digital versus Non-Digital Reference: Ask a Librarian Online and Offline* (ed: Jessamyn West) The Haworth Information Press, an imprint of The Haworth Press, Inc., 2004, pp. xvii-xviii. Single or multiple copies of this article are available for a fee from The Haworth Document Delivery Service [1-800-HAWORTH, 9:00 a.m. - 5:00 p.m. (EST). E-mail address: docdelivery@haworthpress.com].

ing degrees of experience. While the researchers were sometimes good at answering questions, they were almost never librarians. The interface–which allowed for no real reference interview and very little back and forth between question asker and answerer–was clearly designed with ease of use in mind, but ease of use primarily for the customer or casual browser and not for the workers.

Ranganathan tells us to always save the time of the user, but when you are trying to sell staff on a new technique, their comfort level with the software, interface, and implementation of the new tools must also be carefully considered if your project is to succeed.

This volume is arranged thematically with the first section devoted to both traditional reference, as compared and contrasted to digital reference, as well as current e-mail reference projects. The second section consists of the how-to essays, librarians discussing implementation and actual use of digital reference tools and systems. And we finish up with a few more philosophical essays with some discussion of how to think about these new tools and the new paradigm they foist on us, rightly or wrongly.

All of these authors gave generously of their time and efforts, for which I am deeply grateful. Additionally Dr. Bill Katz was a pleasure to interact with and made the article-wrangling process that much easier. I hope you find something here to assist you in your own libraries.

Jessamyn West

SECTION ONE:
THE OLD versus THE NEW

Have(n't) We Been Here Before?
Lessons from Telephone Reference

M. Kathleen Kern

SUMMARY. Telephone reference services have been present in libraries for over seventy-five years. Chat reference services are a very recent addition to library services. Telephone and chat reference share some characteristics and the future of chat reference may be seen through an examination of the history of telephone reference. This article will examine issues of policy, staffing, and technology for telephone and chat reference. *[Article copies available for a fee from The Haworth Document Delivery Service: 1-800-HAWORTH. E-mail address: <docdelivery@haworthpress. com> Website: <http://www.HaworthPress.com> © 2004 by The Haworth Press, Inc. All rights reserved.]*

M. Kathleen Kern is Assistant Reference Librarian, Central Reference Services, University of Illinois at Urbana-Champaign Library, 1408 West Gregory Drive, Urbana, IL 61801 (E-mail: katkern@uiuc.edu).

[Haworth co-indexing entry note]: "Have(n't) We Been Here Before? Lessons from Telephone Reference." Kern, M. Kathleen. Co-published simultaneously in *The Reference Librarian* (The Haworth Information Press, an imprint of The Haworth Press, Inc.) No. 85, 2004, pp. 1-17; and: *Digital versus Non-Digital Reference: Ask a Librarian Online and Offline* (ed: Jessamyn West) The Haworth Information Press, an imprint of The Haworth Press, Inc., 2004, pp. 1-17. Single or multiple copies of this article are available for a fee from The Haworth Document Delivery Service [1-800-HAWORTH, 9:00 a.m. - 5:00 p.m. (EST). E-mail address: docdelivery@haworthpress.com].

http://www.haworthpress.com/web/REF
© 2004 by The Haworth Press, Inc. All rights reserved.
Digital Object Identifer: 10.1300/J120v41n85_01

1

KEYWORDS. Telephone reference, virtual reference, chat reference, library history, reference service, service models

Everyone needs facts and they can be obtained easily–and quickly–from your public library. Perhaps you want to know. . . . It doesn't matter what you want to know, librarians will try to find the answer. It doesn't even matter when you want it, the library is open. . . . And you don't have to come to the library in person. . . .[1]

INTRODUCTION

These words are from a 1956 advertisement for a library telephone service, yet they read now like they could have been written to advertise a virtual reference service provided by the latest online chat technology.

I work at a library that has had an online chat reference service for two years. Every time that someone enters our queue, the software makes a ringing sound, just like a telephone. Not a new program-your-own-sound cell phone, but an old-fashioned, ringing, telephone. For two years I have felt like this should remind us all that in many ways chat reference services are like telephone reference services.

The telephone is old technology and its use for library reference services is also long-standing. In many ways it lies forgotten in the literature, a "been there, doing that" service which does not merit fresh reflection. Chat, on the other hand, is new and exciting and invites reflection and analysis. It is time for the old to bring light to the new. What does the past literature of telephone reference say about clientele, staffing, trends, and policies that we can use to inform the development of the future of chat reference services?

MINDING THE P's AND Q's:
PATRONS, QUESTIONS, AND PARAMETERS

Who

By extending the library outside of the walls, telephone reference invited patrons from outside of the immediate community. Libraries most often have defined affiliate patrons; those who can borrow their books and use their services. While many libraries will provide reference assistance to walk-in patrons, at least by the default of not asking for affili-ation, their policies may exclude providing telephone assistance to non-affiliate patrons. The purpose of these policies is to preserve lim-ited library resources for patrons who provide the tax base, tuition dol-lars, or corporate revenue.

Early on, libraries marketed their telephone reference services to businessmen.[2] This bias was both cultural and economically driven. Businessmen were thought of as people with serious questions, and also with serious community influence. In the 1970s Information and Refer-ral (I & R) services reflected libraries' growing concern with social is-sues and reaching a broader, and often less affluent, patron community.

Libraries have long been concerned with how to handle the influx of telephone queries for non-affiliates. A 1975 study from the University of British Columbia, University of Victoria, and Simon Fraser Univer-sity[3] reported that 12.7% of their requests during the study period were received via telephone. Of the requests received via telephone, 38.7% were from "visitors," 56.7% were from students/faculty, and 4.6% were from users of unknown affiliation. In contrast, visitors represented only 11% of all in-person reference inquiries during the same study. The study concludes that "Financial considerations may in future force aca-demic libraries to re-examine priorities . . ." and "Further study of tele-phone inquiries might be justified."[4]

What

Appropriate audience for telephone reference was not the only ser-vice question. What kinds of questions were acceptable for telephone reference became a growing concern, particularly during the 1950s with the growing popularity of radio quiz shows and trivia contests.[5] A sur-vey in 1950 concluded that "Three out of four of the 25 libraries sur-veyed said that they did not answer quiz questions."[6] In articles as far apart as 50 years, homework assistance was also seen as a problematic category of questions for the telephone reference service.[7] Causes of concern were overload on the service, inappropriateness of providing in-depth assistance by telephone, and problems of providing answers for questions with indeterminate or alternate answers.

These questions were still of concern 30 years later when Rosemarie Riechel wrote her book *Improving Telephone Information and Refer-ence Service in Public Libraries.*[8] She advocated a more evenhanded approach to these categories of questions, stating that "Times have changed, though, and the more common belief is that these [homework, puzzle, quiz, medical, and legal] questions should be dealt with in some way."[9] She advocated flexible policies, and a positive experience for the user. Riechel's advice not withstanding, libraries remained varied in their approaches. For some, the telephone continued to be seen as a limited method of reference communication as reflected in the University of Virginia's 1994 Telephone Reference Service Policy.[10] This example policy discouraged providing in-depth and research assistance via telephone and stipulated that "Normally, telephone service is appropriate for only factual or referral queries."

Edward Riedinger predicted that telephone reference in academic libraries would change as information became more automated and widely available. With more information available to the patron, "Academic libraries at all levels are going to find telephone inquiries becoming more complex due to the density of reference content they include."[11] This short article seems almost prophetic as we read the words "[The user] could be looking at the same catalog screen as the librarian." With the co-browsing capabilities of some chat reference software, how much more complex and information dense might our chat reference interactions be than our telephone reference interactions? How will changes in technology affect the types of questions that we can (or are expected to) field, and what will be the implications for staffing our chat reference services?

Meaning for the Future

Libraries fear that chat will create more questions than they can answer and generate more questions from non-affiliate patrons. Libraries may try to define an affiliate group for chat reference and publicize this policy. Asking patrons to identify their affiliation as part of the chat reference form may allow reference librarians to queue non-affiliates or be prepared to state policy about the use of the chat services. Some libraries may even opt to require users to authenticate with a patron identification number before entering the chat reference service. It must be remembered that this latter method would effectively bar non-affiliate patrons with questions about a library's collections, policies, or services.

The scary picture of thousands of information hungry non-affiliates knocking at our virtual doors may not be accurate. In contrast to the historical examples already mentioned above, a University of California study which focused solely on telephone reference concluded that "In view of the total amount of staff time calculated . . . the area of telephone reference service may be too small to warrant further investigation."[12] If staff time devoted to assisting non-affiliates seems substantial, individual libraries or consortiums may want to examine their own transactions to help establish appropriate policy. An early chat study from the University of Illinois at Urbana-Champaign found that questions from the general public accounted for 5.6% of the questions asked via the chat Ask-A-Librarian service.[13] While another 15.7% did not identify an affiliation, the authors felt that, based on the context of the questions asked, these were mostly affiliate users. More than half of the questions asked by non-affiliates concerned the collections or policies of the University of Illinois Library.[14]

Before turning away non-affiliate chat patrons wholesale, we should examine the extent of the resources that they really use and the types of questions that they ask. Closed door policies may reflect poorly on our individual libraries and our profession as a whole. Guiding non-affiliates to more appropriate services such as their local libraries or subject based Ask-A services may be both helpful and require minimal effort.

There is no consistency in policies and thought regarding what kinds of questions are best answered through chat reference. Some librarians believe that chat reference should be an equivalent service to other reference services while "many librarians suggest that digital reference has already been well determined to be appropriate only for factual questions."[15] Ask-An-Expert services may also serve as a place of referral for libraries wishing to restrict assistance for homework, trivia, or technical questions. Some libraries, such as Baltimore County Public Library,[16] have responded to the need for homework assistance with specialized chat services designed specifically for schoolchildren. As with telephone policies, decisions to exclude or discourage certain types of questions, or to place time limitations, are likely to be local in nature and based on intent of the service, patron constituency, and staffing.

Looking at telephone policies may clarify appropriate non-affiliate and question-type policies for the chat environment. Reference desks do not block out-of-area calls and do not hang up on non-affiliated patrons. However, in the chat environment, non-affiliates may be queued behind affiliate patrons and may be restricted in the kinds of questions that they can ask. Politeness and consistency are called for in turning away patrons; clear, written policies can be helpful in both of these regards.

GEOMETRY OF STAFFING

One Point: Service Convergence

Perhaps the most popular, but least written about, telephone staffing model is to have telephone reference questions answered from the same public service desk as questions from walk-in patrons. In 1983-84, the Association of Research Libraries conducted a survey which found that only 5 of the 89 responding libraries had a separate desk for their telephone inquiries.[17] There is, unfortunately for the history of the profession, a lack of examination into the combined service model. It is perhaps that the norm does not seem in need of investigation or support, or is thought to not make for very provocative articles.

In *A Librarian's Guide to Telephone Reference Service*, Rochelle Yates outlines several reasons and ways to staff a separate telephone reference department. She concludes, however, that there may be reasons to keep walk-in and telephone operations together, namely that librarians may be trained better overall by answering the full range of questions received through both services.

Volume and staffing efficiency also seem likely reasons for a single telephone/in-person service point. A telephone-only desk must be sufficiently busy to justify its existence. Separate service points for in-person and telephone assistance requires staffing at two locations and possibly reference collections at two locations. Libraries must examine if they can afford two service points, where one might be satisfactory.

Two Points Make a Line, Three Points a Plane: Multiple Desks and Tiered Services

Early on, librarians and library researchers found problems with the walk-up desk serving as the telephone desk. In a 1958 "New Techniques" column of *Library Journal*, Robert Dole proposed a telephone department. His fundamental concern is that in-person patrons receive short shrift due to the interruptions of telephone patrons. Telephone patrons also have to wait on hold while in-person patrons are assisted, so he argues that a separate telephone department will be a convenience to both the walk-in and telephoning patron. Greater concern is shown for the in-person patron who has "come five or ten miles" as opposed to the telephone call "placed by a person from the comfort or convenience of their home or office."[18]

While inconvenience to the in-person patron is an underlying concern of most of the articles that support separate telephone reference departments, efficiency and cost-savings through use of paraprofessional staff are other deciding factors. The University of Tennessee, Knoxville, conducted a detailed study which supported a central telephone department staffed by paraprofessionals which answer directional and non-reference questions and would route true reference questions to the reference desk phones.[19]

This sort of tiered telephone service was also in use at public libraries. The Rockford Illinois Public Library started using clerical staff to answer the telephone when they felt that the volume of calls was too high and they "began to interfere with our walk-in clientele."[20] The success of their separated approach to telephone service was (1) that most of the telephone calls were "rather simple" and (2) the clerks staffing the service were "able and intelligent people with the capacity to handle nonroutine situations." Problems did arise when the clerks received questions for which they were not trained and there was uncertainty and reluctance to transfer calls to the reference librarians. Time and training helped with this issue.

An in-depth study was conducted at the Chattanooga-Hamilton Public Library which examined many aspects of telephone reference: types of questions received, subject area, complexity of questions, sources used to answer the questions, and the format of information desired by patron. One of the conclusions of this study was that since two-thirds of all questions asked via telephone were informational in nature, well-trained paraprofessional help could answer the telephones and refer more in-depth or complex questions to reference librarians. The authors did caution the limitation of their study, including that no examination of accuracy had been done and there had been no comparison in any area with questions from walk-in patrons.

Polyhedrons: Collaborations and Consortia

Cooperative telephone reference services were implemented to extend hours, distribute work, or share expertise. While one library might not have had enough traffic or staff to handle extended telephone reference hours, two or more libraries sharing a service were able to make it work, if at least for awhile. Cooperative services seemed especially popular in the late 1960s and early 1970s. The structure of these services was varied, from equal sharing to provision of service by one larger library for a region or entire state.

Berkeley and Oakland Public Libraries were one such cooperative, with each library "taking turns with answering the night phone."[21] This service was cut back and then eliminated in 1991 due to budget cuts.

Peter Bury recommended that library systems in Illinois start a "Telephone Reference Referral Service."[22] As Bury envisioned it, this service would allow member libraries to send questions that they could not answer to the system headquarters or a designated library in the library system or consortium. Librarians and collections at the systems headquarters would be able to answer more difficult questions and any that could not be answered at the systems headquarters would be escalated to one of the four Illinois "research and reference centers" which were designated at that time. For Bury, this tiered service provided access to the collections and expertise of these larger libraries.

Library Line was a venture by the Connecticut State Library to provide reference services to patrons throughout the state. This service was toll-free, accepted calls 24 hours a day (with the assistance of an answering machine) and at times handled 500 calls a day.[23] Maryland ran Night Owl, an after-hours telephone service starting in 1990. Like the Connecticut service, Maryland's Night Owl was operated by a single library (Enoch Pratt Free Library) but available to callers throughout the state.

Some of the challenges to librarians staffing the Maryland service were local questions and questions about a specific library's collections.[24] Another challenge to collaborative telephone service was funding. Berkeley and Oakland's service fell victim to budget cuts but other libraries had plans for survival. Arlington Heights (IL) had the first Night Owl service and found continued funding through offering its night-time telephone reference as a subscription service to other libraries.[25]

Appropriateness of collaborative telephone reference services was in question, even when funding was not at issue. The Maryland Night Owl service was careful to not have questions from the night service answered the next day at the Pratt library; rather, patrons were referred back to their local libraries for daytime assistance. It was important not to be seen as competing with the local libraries.

Meaning for the Future

Staffing for chat reference can be a challenge. At the Virtual Reference Discussion Group held at the ALA Midwinter Meeting 2003, several existing staffing variations were discussed including: separate chat/remote reference service point, single desk for all reference services, librarians staffing chat from their offices, and librarians staffing chat from home (nights and weekends). Most libraries also reported no increase in staff to cover chat service, only an increase in the number of hours spent by each librarian providing reference service. For libraries with a separate chat "desk," some libraries mandated that each librarian staff the service and at least one library let the librarians volunteer for hours. Some libraries used chat consortia and collaborative agreements to handle overflow questions or to distribute the staffing across many libraries to lessen the workload for any one library.[26]

The variety of staffing models is possibly greater than it was for telephone reference. Technology facilitates some of the new models with support of cooperative staffing arrangements that are transparent to the user and consortial subscriptions to online resources. Some chat software programs also allow transferring of patrons between librarians so that a tiered chat service can be operated like the two-desk model.

Ideally, chat reference should be as well-integrated into the existing reference services as are telephone reference services. If we view chat reference as necessary and likely to endure, we must support chat reference as such and not as an ad hoc service. Some libraries currently have more limited hours of reference for their chat service than for their other reference services. If staffing is the primary reason for short hours of service, then libraries should examine if there is a more optimal staffing model which will support a more robust service and not over-extend the patience of staff or patrons. Our libraries are diverse institutions with diverse organizational models. It is improbable that there will be one single staffing model for chat reference that is best for all libraries to adopt.

Many of the same considerations apply to staffing of chat reference services as to telephone reference services. A single service point for in-person, telephone, and chat reference might be chosen for economy, balancing workflow, and best development and sharing of expertise. Criticism of this model is likely to be the same as it was for the single point telephone/in-person desk; it may be difficult to juggle patrons and patrons may not appreciate waiting while other patrons are helped via other modes of communication. It may be outmoded, however, to think of the remote patron as less important than the in-person patron. Patrons have many reasons for accessing the library remotely and online resources have made it possible to use both library resources and services from remote locations. Even if the library does not give priority to one mode of communication over another, patrons' reactions to waiting must be considered.

The two-desk, tiered service, model may be chosen to minimize impact on in-person service. Chat might be handled from its own remote services desk or from the same service desk as other remote services such as telephone and e-mail. This would eliminate the awkwardness of explaining to an in-person that you have a chat patron you are helping. It might also reduce staff anxiety about juggling various modes of communication. A tiered model may allow a library to utilize paraprofessionals to staff chat reference if there is a software and organizational support for seamlessly referring chat patrons to a reference librarian. An examination of questions asked via chat may support or refute a tiered model of staffing, but types of questions are likely to vary between institutions.

Care needs to be taken to protect staff when an additional service point is set up for chat. Librarians staffing from their offices may find that the time available for off-desk responsibilities is decreased. If a new service point is added without additional staff and librarians take on extra hours to cover the service, it will cut into time for other responsibilities and the additional desk hours may result in reference burn-out.

As with the telephone, collaborations and consortia are being used to expand hours of service and at times to provide 24/7 live chat reference. Some implementations might use librarians across many libraries and others might use staffing contracted with vendors to provide after-hours service. There are many considerations to be asked in forming or joining a reference consortia: how much time and money will each library contribute, is it appropriate for staff at other libraries (or vendors) to answer your patrons questions, will all librarians have access to the same resources, and what is the referral mechanism between libraries?

Rochelle Yates' assessment of the complexities of staffing telephone reference seems to ring true for the staffing of chat reference. "There is no one, right, answer to this question of separating the telephone from the general reference area. There is no one, right form of telephone information service that will work in every library. Nonetheless, there is definitely such a thing as good service and poor service."[27]

INNOVATION AROUND EVERY CORNER

Telephones have been around for more than 125 years and have been present in libraries since at least 1876.[28] Early use was for connecting branch libraries and not for reference services to the public. The earliest innovation per se was to open up the telephone lines to the public. Today it is difficult to imagine library reference without the telephone; it is so ubiquitous. While technological basics of the telephone have remained the same, there were a few innovations in the intervening 125 years. Some of these were technological innovations and some were service innovations; some of them left their mark and some of them, well, got disconnected.

Whither Technology?

A 1936 advertisement in *Library Journal* for a telephone switchboard announces it as a time-saving device for the library information service. Calls are first answered by a library assistant who can direct them to the appropriate library department, thus saving the caller misdirection. The library assistant is referred to in the advertisement as an "interpreter-hostess,"[29] a term which could indicate either the first occurrence of call screening or of a tiered information/reference service.

Teletype machines, teleprinters, and TWX transmit messages via telephone lines or radio relays.[30] These systems found their greatest use in Interlibrary Lending operations, but also experienced a period of popularity (or at least promotion) for use in reference transactions. The teletype and its cousins were made obsolete by the fax machine and then by Internet communications.

Facsimile transmission via telephone lines was pioneered in the 1920s.[31] Throughout the 1970s articles in library science still regarded fax transmittal as something out of the ordinary. The technology did not become widely used in libraries until the early 1980s, when better and cheaper technology made it more commonplace. Like the teletype machines that they eclipsed, fax machines found their widest application in ILL operations. One consortium expected a high level of fax use for shared reference (between libraries) and attributed lack of use to reference librarians not being comfortable with calling upon one another.[32] Another group of libraries did find a successful use for the fax in a reference setting. Ten Illinois libraries set up a network to share CD-ROM databases networked to fax machines. Librarians at Library X faxed a request for a database search of a CD-ROM located at Library Y. Library Y performed the search and using special software, the search results were faxed from the CD-ROM database directly to Library X. The cited benefits of the system were shared cost of CD-ROM databases and shared searching expertise.[33]

These two services were both library-to-library uses of the fax in a reference setting. Patron-to-librarian fax services do not appear much in the literature. At the same time, I have never worked at a library that did not accept faxed reference requests from patrons. Faxed reference requests fit more neatly into the category of reference correspondence (remember receiving letters with stamps?). The technology resembles the telephone, but the communication is asynchronous and therefore not subject to quite the same issues of staffing as telephone reference, although the policy and patron affiliation issue remain.

One notable service started in 1972 combined the telephone with the television to deliver reference. Telephone requests came into the Mobile Public Library's Moorer Regional Branch and reference staff transmitted images of "diagrams, graphs, maps, recipes, and similar items" to patrons using the "For Information" cable TV channel. A surveillance camera located in a study carrel was all the equipment that was needed. The service was to "be maintained indefinitely, unless public demand for it slackens off."[34] There seem to be no published reports on the success of this service.

A more lasting innovation was the telephone answering machine. Answering machines and voicemail are commonplace enough today not to engender much thought. In 1970, College and Research Libraries published an article that gave a lot of ideas on how to maximize this piece of equipment. The automatic answering machine could extend the library's hours by giving out routine information such as hours, and also by recording questions for later answer by reference staff. The answering machine could be used not only when the library is closed, but when it is staffed only with students, thus alleviating the patron of incorrectly answered questions and the librarian of poorly written telephone messages. So, like all technologies, this one has embedded issues of staffing and policy.

24/7: The Early Years

The telephone answering machine was not the only way that the library could use the telephone to extend its hours of operation. Several libraries at least experimented with increasing telephone reference hours beyond the normal hours of reference operation. (Information on the start of service is more prevalent than information on the end of services.)

Maryland's Night Owl service, which was mentioned earlier, operated until midnight, Monday through Friday. Duke wrote in support of the Night Owl service that "Adding 'non-traditional' services such as after hours reference is another way that libraries can keep in step with the rest of the world."[35]

Boulder Public Library in Colorado used University of Colorado students paying off federal grants to answer its telephone reference service from the hours of 9-11 p.m., two hours past the library's usual closing time. The students were trained in basic ready reference sources and more complicated questions were referred to professional staff to be answered the next day. It was believed that only 20 percent of the calls fell outside of the area of ready reference.

An even more ambitious project was implemented by the California State College at Stanislaus, which expanded its telephone reference service to 24 hours a day. Librarians answered questions from their homes after hours, using duplicate copies of ready reference works. Librarians were given compensation for late night staffing through time off. The service met with favorable response from students and faculty, and was used 24 times during a five-week evaluation period. During the evaluation period, librarians went into the library three times to answer the question. Fifteen of the requests were for help with search strategies. Most of the calls came in when the library was open, but not staffed with a reference librarian. Only two calls came in during times when the library was closed. In the words of the library director, "the librarians considered it 'a useful service at little cost in time and trouble.' "[36]

Meaning for the Future

Innovations never occur as islands; there is always an isthmus connecting one change to another. A change in technology necessarily brings with it considerations of the impact on and potentials for service. Changes in service effect staff and patrons and thus must influence procedure and policy. As we look at innovations in telephone reference we may recognize the terrain. Technological changes in and around chat reference software are numerous. Some have already fizzled and others are still developing. Twenty-four/seven reference is not as new as some of us may think.

The teletype and the facsimile machine were long-lasting technologies. However, the impact on reference services was, for most libraries, not as voluminous as anticipated. Likewise, some libraries report that chat reference volume is less than anticipated.[37] An important *difference* to remember is that fax and teletype are asynchronous services (perhaps closer in analogy to e-mail), while chat requires people at both ends of the transmission. If we are to expect a great return on our investment in chat reference, then we must make provision for after-hours contact, and not just leave a dead line. Libraries may do this by directing chat patrons to e-mail when the chat service is closed.

What is more applicable here about teletype and facsimile technologies is that they were precursors to more advanced technologies. E-mail (and chat) has largely taken the place of these technologies in reference services. Television, on the other hand, did not have the same endurance as a reference tool. The answering machine, or voicemail, is still in place in libraries, at least as a method of providing hours of operation. Some libraries utilize a switchboard concept (using more modern technology) by funneling calls through a receptionist or an information desk. Technology changes, but can leave its imprint. We need to work to employ chat wisely for our patrons and for our staff. Will we know which chat technologies are appropriate for our patrons? Will we know when it is time to move on to the next technology? Can we foresee and respond to the evolution of technologies without being caught up in the fads?

The same principles and questions are true for innovation in services. Twenty-four/seven is a catchy idea. Working from home and being on call may be less of a catchy idea after a year or two into a service. What is marketable is not always what is desirable. If the California State College 24/7 telephone service did not get more use after a few semesters, it was quite likely the target of budget cuts, or reorganization of priorities, which surely disappointed a few patrons. While that is speculation, it is not really far-flung to say that in the current economy, it will take more than glitz to keep a service staffed and vital. Libraries that want a robust chat service might want to examine their hours of chat operation. By all reports, the patrons that use the chat services rave. We need to evaluate and examine our operations. What hours will reach our users? Does perceived need for longer hours actually result in expected use of the service?

It may be easy to look back critically at some of the past innovations in telephone reference and analyze their shortcomings. That some of these ideas are being recycled points to an enduring appeal. The concept behind the television reference channel is revived through such technologies as online video where the patron can see the librarian or a printed book, as well as through co-browsing where the patron can see the same web page as the librarian. Twenty-four/seven reference is being revitalized by technologies that: support working from home, collaboration between libraries, and patron access to library resources from any computer at any time. What remains to be proven is whether these advances to technology make these innovations more supportable. By examining the "what worked and what didn't" of telephone reference innovations we can hopefully start chat innovations at a point which is more informed and more advanced. A less than perfect innovation in the past does not indicate that a similar future innovation will fail, but it should be something from which we learn.

CONCLUSION

Examination of telephone reference history reveals policies and practices as diverse as our libraries. It also reveals trends in services and innovation which continue or recycle from one technology to the next. We must open up our local memories as well. Articles about telephone reference only hint at the variety and breadth of telephone reference services. Most libraries did not formally write up their experiences, but local files and people's memories may tell us what was done at our own institutions and help us with new decisions that affect our patrons and our staff.

Reading many of the articles and treatises on telephone reference, I could almost imagine them to be writing about chat reference instead. So, as a parting thought, please consider these examples:

> It has been established that telephone [chat] reference is important as a means of extending the use of public libraries as reference agencies. Telephone [Chat] reference increases the quality of service by providing access to the library's resources to a remote population.[38]

> The general plan of telephone [chat] service offered depends upon the organization of the library, its size, its budget, and the number of inquiries usually received.[39]

REFERENCES AND NOTES

1. Sarah Rebecca Reed, "1946-1956 Public Library Reference Services," *Library Journal* 82 (January 15, 1957), 131-137.

2. Emily Garnett, "Reference Service by Telephone," *Library Journal* 61 (April 15, 1936), 909.

3. "TRIUL Survey of Reference Use, October 23-29, 1975" in *SPEC Kit #73 on External User Services* (Washington, DC: Association of Research Libraries, 1981), 37-60.

4. Ibid. p. 43.

5. Elizabeth Bond, "Some Problems of Telephone Reference Service," *Library Journal* 82 (January 15, 1957), 133.

6. Howard Samuelson, "Milwaukee Installs Phone Service Desk," *Library Journal* 75 (October 1, 1950), 1602-1603.

7. Emily Garnett, p. 910 and Riedinger, p. 673.

8. Rosemarie Riechel, *Improving Telephone Information and Reference Service in Public Libraries* (Hamden, CT: Library Professional Publications, 1987).

9. Ibid. p. 20.

10. University of Virginia, "Alderman Library Reference Department Telephone Reference Service Policy" in *SPEC Kit #203: Reference Service Policies in ARL Libraries,* edited by Anna L. DeMiller (Washington DC: Association of Research Libraries, 1994), 113-114.

11. Edward Riedinger, "Telephone Information Service," *C&RL News* 50 (September 1989), 672-673.

12. Anne R. Oja, *A Survey of Reference Requests Received by Telephone with Tabulations by Affiliation of Caller: A Report of Findings* (California: University of California Systemwide Administration, 1978), 7-8.

13. Jo Kibbee, David Ward, and Wei Ma, "Virtual Services, Real Data: Results of a Pilot Study," *Reference Services Review* 22 (2002), 25-36.

14. Ibid. p. 33.

15. Joseph Janes and Chrystie Hill, "Finger on the pulse: librarians describe evolving reference practice in an increasingly digital world," *Reference & User Services Quarterly* 42 (2002), 54-66.

16. Joseph Thompson, "After School and Online," *Library Journal* 128 (January 2003), 35-8.

17. Frank R. Allen and Rita H. Smith, "A Survey of Telephone Inquiries: Case Study and Operational Impact in an Academic Library Reference Department," *RQ* 32 (Spring 1993), 384.

18. Robert H. Rolf, "Let's Consider a Telephone Reference Department," *Library Journal* 83 (January 1, 1958), 50-53.

19. Frank R. Allen and Rita H. Smith, "A Survey of Telephone Inquiries: Case Study and Operational Impact in an Academic Library Reference Department," *RQ* 32 (Spring 1993), 383-91.

20. Richard W. Shellman, "Clerical Help Meets the Public," *RQ* 12 (Fall 1972), 58.

21. "Afterhours Reference by Phone Popular," *Library Journal* 95 (March 15, 1970), 972.

22. Peter Bury, "Reference '67: The Suburban Library," *Illinois Libraries* 49 (April 1967), 249-251.

23. "Library Line," *American Libraries*, 6 (January 1975), 19.

24. Deborah C. Duke, "Night Owl: Maryland's After-hours Reference Service," *Public Libraries* 33 (May/June 1994), 145-148.

25. Ibid. p. 145.

26. Unpublished minutes. RUSA MARS Virtual Reference Discussion Group, ALA Midwinter, Philadelphia Sat., Jan. 25, 2003 4:30 PM-5:30 PM Overture Room, Doubletree Hotel.

27. Rochelle Yates, p. 5-6.

28. Justin Wilson, "From the President's Address," *Library Journal* 2 (1876), 22.

29. "The Switchboard," *Library Journal* 61 (April 15, 1936), 330.

30. "Teleprinter." *Encyclopedia Britannica* 2003 *Encyclopedia Britannica Online*.10 Apr, 2003 <http://search.eb.com/eb/article?eu=73455>.

31. "Telephone and Telephone System." *Encyclopedia Britannica* 2003 *Encyclopedia Britannica Online*.10 Apr, 2003 <http://search.eb.com/eb/article?eu=119002>.

32. Mark Wilson and Helen A. Gordon. "How to Set Up a Telefacsimile Network–The Pennsylvania Libraries' Experience," *Online* 12 (May 1988), 15.

33. Diana Fitzwater and Bernard Fradkin, "CD-ROM + Fax = Shared Reference Resource," *American Libraries* 19 (May 1988), 385.

34. "Video Reference Service Set Up at Alabama Library." *Library Journal* 97 (June 1, 1972), 2031.

35. Ibid. p. 148.

36. "California State College's 24-hours Reference Service," *Library Journal* 98 (November 15, 1973), 3336.

37. Brian Kenney. "Live, digital reference: a close look at libraries' exciting new service. (An LJ Round Table)," *Library Journal* 127 (October 1, 2002), 46.

38. Rosemarie Reichel, p. 114.

39. Emily Garnett, p. 909.

E-Mail Reference
as Substitute for Library Receptionist

Susan M. Braxton
Maureen Brunsdale

SUMMARY. The authors explore the historical development of e-mail reference services in general, and report on the evolution of this service in their own library. Based on evidence from their own service and from reports in the literature, they propose a connection between e-mail reference service and broader library services including circulation, interlibrary loan, and even acquisitions, through which the reference librarian receives questions traditionally directed elsewhere. The e-ref button presents an unexpected avenue of librarian-to-librarian communication, both within and beyond one's home institution. Implications are discussed. *[Article copies available for a fee from The Haworth Document Delivery Service: 1-800-HAWORTH. E-mail address: <docdelivery@haworthpress. com> Website: <http://www.HaworthPress.com> © 2004 by The Haworth Press, Inc. All rights reserved.]*

KEYWORDS. E-mail reference, reference services, academic libraries

Susan M. Braxton (E-mail: smbraxt@ilstu.edu) is Science Reference Librarian and Maureen Brunsdale (E-mail: Maureen@exchange1.mlb.ilstu.edu) is Access Services Librarian, both at Milner Library, Illinois State University, Campus Box 8900, Normal, IL 61790-8900.

[Haworth co-indexing entry note]: "E-Mail Reference as Substitute for Library Receptionist." Braxton, Susan M., and Maureen Brunsdale. Co-published simultaneously in *The Reference Librarian* (The Haworth Information Press, an imprint of The Haworth Press, Inc.) No. 85, 2004, pp. 19-31; and: *Digital versus Non-Digital Reference: Ask a Librarian Online and Offline* (ed: Jessamyn West) The Haworth Information Press, an imprint of The Haworth Press, Inc., 2004, pp. 19-31. Single or multiple copies of this article are available for a fee from The Haworth Document Delivery Service [1-800-HAWORTH, 9:00 a.m. - 5:00 p.m. (EST). E-mail address: docdelivery@haworthpress.com].

http://www.haworthpress.com/web/REF
© 2004 by The Haworth Press, Inc. All rights reserved.
Digital Object Identifer: 10.1300/J120v41n85_02

INTRODUCTION

Electronic reference services have evolved alongside the technological revolution. While technological transformations have seemed to intersect with the human side of librarianship at a feverish pace, the metamorphosis of electronic reference services has been more gradual, spanning several decades and technologies and beginning with the telephone. This paper traces the evolution in general and in one academic library, and characterizes one professional's experiences with e-mail reference services. While most of the work of e-mail reference experienced at Milner Library may be actual reference work, there are times when e-mail reference serves as a "library switchboard" with a librarian as receptionist linking patrons to the appropriate departments.

A HISTORY OF E-MAIL REFERENCE SERVICE IN LIBRARIES

Developed as an office automation tool, e-mail was initially adopted by the private sector. The literature of the 1970s is rife with descriptions of electronic mail software and predictions of eventual widespread adoption (Hiltz and Turoff 1978). Choate suggested that libraries in the private sector were able to take advantage of new online technologies better because they were not hampered financially. In fact, the earliest use of e-mail for direct information transfer between information professionals and their patrons appears to have occurred in corporate information centers. For example, GTE's information centers offered e-mail reference services in 1980 (Eager 1981). Also in 1980, Information on Demand and The Information Store, two information companies, were using e-mail to communicate with clients (Josephine 1980, 42). Document requests were one of the primary uses by patrons/clients of e-mail at that time (Josephine 1980, 42). See Table 1 for a chronology of e-mail and related technologies that have influenced and facilitated digital reference in libraries.

Libraries outside the corporate setting were not far behind their corporate counterparts. Libraries initially employed e-mail for interlibrary communication to facilitate transactions such as interlibrary loan; e-mail was implemented as a cheaper, more convenient alternative than telephone or surface mail communication between borrowing and lending libraries (see De Gennaro 1987, 9; Sloan 1990, 1; Dewey 1989, 9; and Dialog's . . . 1985, 31, for example). Proprietary systems which re-

TABLE 1. A Chronology of Events Relevant to the Development of Reference Services via Electronic Mail

Year	Event
1969	Advanced Research Project Agency Network (ARPANET) established, laying the foundation for the Internet (Spencer 1997, 162).
1972	First e-mail message sent from one computer to another (Robson 2001, 274). First computer-to-computer chat session takes place (Zakon 2003).
1973	Wireless communication allows addition of Hawaii and London sites to the ARPANET (Hauben 2001, 51). ARPA study shows 75% of ARPANET traffic is e-mail (Zakon 2003).
1974	System Development Corporation pioneers e-mail for libraries with an electronic ordering service (Maildrop) for online searchers in ORBIT (Carr 1981, 94), but service does not offer two-way communication (Josephine 1980, 42).
1979	DIALOG introduces DialOrder, which provided electronic document delivery for dialog searchers (Carr 1981, 94).
1980	California Library Authority for Systems and Services (CLASS) contracts with OnTyme for its own version of their e-mail system, which becomes known as OnTyme II (Bruman 1985, 57). This represents the largest library e-mail system effort of its day and connects libraries throughout the west (Electronic . . . 1982, 2).
1980	GTE corporate information centers offer e-mail reference to patrons within the organization on a limited basis (Eager 1981).
1982	E-mail is the "fastest growing technology in libraries," with uses including interlibrary loan requesting and referral of reference questions (Electronic . . . 1982, 1).
1983	MILNet splits from ARPANET, which continues as the scientific and educational portion of the original network (Hauben 2001, 52).
1983	ALL OUT Library proposed (Sleeth & LaRue 1983).
January 1984	ALANET begins operation; network allows librarians to consult on reference questions (Lee 1984, 64; Electronic . . . 1984, 31).
May 1984	University of Washington Medical Library begins e-mail reference service in May (Howard & Jankowski 1986, 41).
September 1984	Electronic Access to Reference Service (EARS) goes online in September at the Health Sciences Library at the University of Maryland at Baltimore (Weise & Borgendale 1986, 303).
1985	DIALMAIL introduced; network allows librarians to consult on reference questions (Dialog's . . . 1985, 12).
1985	America Online founded (Shields 2001, 25).
1987	"Backbone of the Internet" established by NSF with the help of IBM (Spencer 1997, 273).
1988	Internet Relay Chat (IRC) invented (Zakon 2003).
1989	Tim Berners-Lee invents the first browser and pens *Information Management: A Proposal* which describes a vision for the World Wide Web (Dunker 2001, 844 and Woodford 2001, 119).
1990	ARPANET decommissioned (Hauben 2001, 52).
1992	Incipient World Wide Web consists of fewer than 100 servers in 1992 (Dunker 2001, 843).
1993	Development of Mosaic browser leads to dramatic growth of the World Wide Web (Woodford 2001, 859).
April 1994	Netscape Communications Corporation founded (Spencer 1997, 300). Yahoo! begins life as a directory called "Jerry's Guide to the World Wide Web" (Woodford 2001, 859).
1995	More than 1 million servers make up the World Wide Web (Dunker 2001, 843).
March 1995	Internet Public Library created; foremost function is reference service to the Internet patron base (Serving . . . 1996, 122).
1995	Milner Library's e-mail reference service established.
1999	An estimated 45% of academic libraries employ digital reference service; all of this is found to be in the form of e-mail and not chat (Janes et al. 1999, 145-48).
2000	An estimated 45% of master's level institution's libraries found to be providing digital reference service (White 2001, 175).
2001	Milner Library begins participating in Ready for Reference, a consortial chat reference service.
2003	Approximately 48% of the libraries of postsecondary educational institutions in Illinois offer e-mail reference service.

mained incompatible and unconnected to one another into the mid-1990s (Robson 2001, 273) may have hampered the utility of e-mail for the general public and for libraries as well. However, networks allowing e-mail communication were common at least in larger academic institutions in the 1980s, and were a promising means of communication in academic research libraries (The Use . . . 1988).

Early uses of e-mail for reference also involved librarian-to-librarian communication. Librarian networks, such as ALANET implemented in 1984 (Lee 1984, 64) and DIALMAIL implemented in 1985 (Dialog's . . . 1985, 12) allowed consultation among librarians on difficult reference questions, but did not facilitate patron-to-librarian communication.

Sleeth and LaRue's ALL OUT library recommendations included two-way message transmission, one function of which would be the ability of patrons to ask questions "answerable by brief ready reference responses" (Sleeth and LaRue 1983, 595). Reports of e-mail reference services in academic libraries began to appear soon thereafter in the literature, but not in great numbers.

Apparently, medical and health science libraries in academic institutions were among the first non-corporate libraries to implement e-mail reference service allowing patron-to-librarian communication. The University of Washington Medical Library launched their service in May 1984 (Howard and Jankowski 1986, 41); however, the authors reported 95% of contacts during the first 10 months of the service were photocopy requests (Howard and Jankowski 1986, 42). In September 1984, the Health Sciences Library at the University of Maryland, Baltimore, implemented EARS (Electronic Access to Reference Service) (Weise and Borgendale 1986, 303). EARS allowed patrons to make reference queries or request various library services via e-mail, using terminals either on or off campus. The authors reported that use was dominated by requests for photocopy services, although some reference questions were asked (Weise and Borgendale 1986, 303).

In 1987, Buckland advocated adding e-mail communication to the increasingly ubiquitous OPACs maintained by libraries, noting that the existence of the OPAC meant that the necessary technology for e-mail communication between patrons and their libraries was already in place. Buckland's recommendations imply that at that time, e-mail reference was far from commonplace. Whitaker reported in 1989 that "the typical librarian seems not to employ electronic communication in his/ her daily work" citing barriers such as inter-network incompatibility, lack of training, low need for use, and cost. At this time, interlibrary loan continued to be the primary use of e-mail in libraries (Whitaker 1989, 360).

Throughout the 1990s e-mail became increasingly common. The World Wide Web was born and grew (see Table 1), facilitating electronic access both to resources and to other people. Recreational use of e-mail and chat by the general public through such Internet service providers as America Online grew, and created a population familiar with the technologies now used in digital reference. In March of 1995, the Internet Public Library came online (Serving. . . 1996, 122), offering a model for providing reference service to Internet-based patrons. Also during this period, web directories, search engines, and "Ask An Expert" services which were not associated with libraries proliferated, accompanied by much discussion among librarians (see, for example, Coffman & McGlamery 2000, and Janes et al. 2001).

By May 1999 about 45% of academic libraries provided some form of e-mail reference service according to a survey of academic library web sites. Libraries with digital reference tended to be larger by various measures, to serve schools with more advanced Carnegie classifications (i.e., doctoral or research institutions) (Janes et al. 1999, 145-47), and to serve public rather than private colleges and universities (Janes et al. 1999, 149). Janes reported that 75% of librarians surveyed (at both public and academic libraries) were participating in some form of digital reference service, with only 8% of librarians responding that their service had been in place more than five years. The number participating in digital reference was slightly higher, 83%, for academic librarians only (Janes 2002, 552). In spring of 2000, White examined libraries serving master's level institutions and found that 45% of these libraries offered e-mail reference service (White 2001, 175), which was an increase over the level of 33% found by Janes et al. one year earlier for libraries at master's level institutions (Janes et al. 1999, 147).

While e-mail reference is common, it is by no means universal in academic or other libraries. Librarians have been admonished against allowing their library to be the last to offer e-mail reference (Schneider 2000, 96), and offered instructions for implementation of the service (see, for example, Greene 2002, and Lankes and Kasowitz 1998). In 2001, 13 of 23 (~57%) academic libraries surveyed in Colorado had e-mail reference service, with an additional 3 libraries providing e-mail reference service for distance education students only (Lederer 2001, 57).

In Illinois, there are 136 post-secondary educational institutions, including public and private community colleges, junior colleges, professional schools, colleges, universities, and seminaries (Hoss 2002 and Turlington 1999). As of April 2003, all of the schools had web sites with some link to a library web site or to information about library services, and 66 (48%) of them have a link to, or provide an electronic address for, e-mail reference service. One explanation for the apparent small advance in e-mail reference service since 1999, may be the inclusion of categories of institutions (e.g., junior colleges) which were excluded from the Janes et al.'s (1999, 145-47) survey. Thirteen of the libraries offering e-mail reference service in Illinois also offer chat reference, which does represent an advance as compared to the 1999 study, when no real time chat services were identified (Janes et al. 1999, 148).

HISTORY OF DIGITAL REFERENCE SERVICES IN MILNER LIBRARY

Illinois State University is classified as a Carnegie Doctoral/Research University/Intensive institution, and Milner Library has a rich history of providing reference service to its users. Since opening in 1976, the library has been arranged by subject, with each of its floors focusing on different subject areas. There are five reference desks in the building, four subject specialized desks and one general reference desk, which is on the main floor and faces the main entrance of the library.

Milner Library's involvement with digital reference service began in 1995–before there was a Milner web presence–with the introduction of e-mail reference. When Milner Library's web page came online in the latter half of 1996, a link to the service was introduced. With the increased visibility of e-mail reference provided by the web page, the number of e-mail reference questions jumped dramatically from three questions in 1995 to sixty-five questions in 1996. While this service did not maintain this aggressive growth pattern, the e-mail reference librarian on duty now expects at least a handful of questions daily.

Patrons can submit their questions using a web form (two clicks from our home page). A notice on the form reads: "This service is designed for providing brief answers to factual questions or suggesting appropriate sources. In some cases, questions will be referred to subject specialists. We are not able to perform lengthy research" (Ask A . . . 2002). In addition, Ovid database users also find a link to a web form allowing them to "ask a Milner librarian" in the Ovid interface, which also leads to a web form. Patrons are also provided with a direct e-mail address to the service, in the event the form and their browser do not function together. (There are also mailto links either for the webmaster or for the appropriate librarian on all web pages that make up the Milner Library web site. This librarian has received at least one query forwarded from the Milner webmaster.) There is no restriction on who may use the service, and no technological barrier to submission of questions. Patrons are advised that responses may be expected in 24 hours or less, with the exceptions of weekends and holidays.

Thirty-three professional librarians currently work in Milner Library. Not all reference librarians participate in e-mail reference services at any one time. Participation is voluntary, and varies by the semester as people's work responsibilities shift. Usually, at least 11 professional librarians participate in providing e-mail reference service, and those who take part generally are scheduled for one Monday through Friday period during each semester. The service is currently coordinated by Milner Library's Education/Library Science librarian.

In the spring of 2001 real-time chat reference service was implemented at Milner. Sponsored in part by the Alliance Library System, a library learning community composed of special, school, public, and academic libraries, the pilot service is open to and marketed to patrons throughout the state of Illinois and is available around the clock. A commercial vendor supplies a hosted solution so that participating libraries need not install or maintain any hardware or software. A coordinator from the Alliance Library System arranges staffing for the virtual desk from 8 in the morning until 6 in the evening, Monday through Friday. Each of the participating eight academic libraries decides how many hours the virtual desk will be supported by librarians at each institution. Professionals in the vendor's employ staff the desk overnight and on weekends and holidays. As with the e-mail reference service, participation in the chat service is voluntary. There are currently nine Milner librarians involved with providing this type of service, and they serve shifts of one to several hours per week. There is considerable overlap in the Milner librarians participating in the two digital reference services offered.

An investigation of the questions received through e-mail, and their eventual handling, shows how the e-mail reference button has become a multipurpose access point, mediated by a human being, operating in much the same way that a receptionist desk would, and in much the same way as Milner's general reference desk does. While performing e-mail reference, librarians may forward queries to more appropriate personnel, such as a subject specialist or the access services department. Thus, the patron, rather than experiencing telephone transfers, or referrals to another physical location, and perhaps multiple repetitions of her/his query, simply receives an answer from someone within a specified time. The access point becomes irrelevant to the patron, who only knows that she or he is getting the information requested.

ONE LIBRARIAN'S EXPERIENCE
WITH E-MAIL REFERENCE

We report here on the admittedly limited e-mail reference experience of one of the authors. Eighteen days of e-mail reference service were performed: 17-21 June 2002, 9-13 September 2002, 7 October 2002, 18 December 2002, 7-8 January 2003, and 20-24 January 2003. Records were kept in the form of archived responses to the queries. The number of patrons and queries reported here represent a conservative estimate, as the archiving was not automated, and human error very likely resulted in the loss of some responses.

Over the 18 days, 64 patrons asked 69 queries, for an average of 3.6 patrons and 3.8 queries per day. As might be expected, the number of questions received was lower during the summer and between semesters. During fall and spring semesters, the average number of patrons and queries per day was higher, 4.9 and 5.3 respectively. Traffic on the service suggests an active patron base, which matches the perception of the participating librarians. Faculty, graduate students, undergraduate students and alumni all used the service during the eighteen days of service by this librarian, as well as patrons at large from other states and even other countries.

Of the queries received, 45 were considered reference queries, and almost all of the remaining 24 were questions related to access services. Despite the stated intent of the service, this librarian found that few of the reference questions could be answered with a quick fact or resource suggestion. Nearly half (21) the responses to the 45 reference queries were instructional; that is, rather than merely suggesting an appropriate resource, the response included instructions on how to choose an appropriate resource, how to find it, or how to use it, or all of the above. When the reference philosophy is that of empowering patrons to use resources, as it is in most academic libraries, even the simplest query is an opportunity to offer instruction. Sometimes, those questions which might have been answerable by brief factual responses required covering multiple bases, as the question being asked was not entirely clear. The experience of ambiguous questions has been corroborated by research showing that patrons do not compose better questions when they are e-mailing them (Gross et al. 2001, 4), as has been frequently postulated, even by this librarian.

Referrals from the e-mail reference service to the Milner Library's Access Services Division Head (or alternatively, inquiries made by librarians serving at e-mail reference on behalf of patrons) corroborate the observed frequency of non-reference questions reported above. It is not unusual for this librarian to answer two or three questions per week for the e-mail reference service. Questions cover all services encompassed in Access Services at Milner Library, including course reserves, electronic reserves, circulation and interlibrary loan. Queries range from requests to renew books, to understanding how to place requests on books (either for materials owned locally or through interlibrary loan services), to facilitating e-reserves requests and beyond. It is this librarian's practice to respond to both the person who originated the question, and the librarian who sent forward the e-mail. In this way, all parties become informed of the procedures and policies.

A surprising aspect of the experience has been a number of queries from individuals that could reasonably be expected to have a more appropriate contact at Milner than the e-mail reference link. These include librarians attempting to initiate interlibrary loan transactions, and, incredibly, one publisher representative inquiring after Milner's subscription renewal plans in the wake of the Faxon collapse. Apparently, e-mail reference contact from interlibrary loan librarians is not unusual, prompting one researcher to refer to questions on interlibrary loan posed through the "aska" service as "answer a librarian" (Lederer 2001, 65).

CONCLUSIONS

A majority of librarians (from public and academic libraries combined) agreed that digital technologies make reference "more fun" (Janes 2002, 557). One possible explanation for this perception is that e-mail is the most prevalent form of digital reference, and e-mail reference is a low pressure venue. While librarians may find digital reference more fun, patron satisfaction is not yet known. It is clear that patrons are using Milner's e-mail reference service–and some are even returning to the service–it is not certain that the service is meeting their needs adequately. Forthcoming work by Stoffel (in prep) will address this issue.

E-mail reference is also convenient for both the librarian and the patron, who can ask and answer when the time is available and when the question or answer is on their minds. Even a very rude and impatient e-mail message is not nearly as distressing as a rude, impatient patron right in front of the reference desk. And, even if patrons do not clearly compose their e-mail queries, as has been suggested (Gross et al. 2001, 4), librarians do have the luxury of thinking through their responses. The librarian's written answer can be saved and reread as needed, which is a plus for the patron.

The authors have been privy to various discussions of e-mail's community-building versus distancing impacts–in classes, on listservs, and elsewhere. E-mail reference appears to support the community-building arguments, at least in some respects. E-mail reference makes librarians more visible to patrons who increasingly use online services, such as the OPAC and electronic indexes and journals, from remote locations. E-mail reference keeps librarians in the picture even when the patron never enters the building. As an access point, the e-mail reference form is comfortable and approachable, at least for some users. The patron facing the e-mail reference link will not be put off by a line of patrons ahead of them or by the persona of the librarian on duty, because the queue of digital queries and the librarian are invisible.

E-mail reference may also foster communication among librarians and staff in a library offering the service. E-mail reference librarians may field questions outside their normal area of specialty, and connect with other librarians outside their area of service (e.g., access services, acquisitions). Whereas face to face reference may not leave time for anything other than referral, deeper exploration is often possible when conducting e-mail reference. Although it can turn the participating librarian into a receptionist of sorts, e-mail reference service presents opportunities for networking and learning that may not occur in other reference venues.

Finally, some may perceive that "receptionist duty" at the virtual reference desk is not the work of a professional librarian. However, it should be noted that librarians field a considerable number of questions on the location of the bathroom while serving at the physical reference desk. Thus, the e-mail reference desk is a no less professional position. Alternatives to the librarian on duty fielding all questions and forwarding them as necessary include asking patrons to self-select the type of service needed, using paraprofessional staff to evaluate questions, or using an automated text processing solution to place questions in appropriate queues. None of these solutions is ideal, and at the current level of traffic on Milner's service, far from necessary. Possibly the types of questions being asked of the e-mail reference service indicate that the information needed is not easily found on the academic library's web site. The authors do not find it burdensome to answer the frequently asked questions, and believe that some patrons may be reassured by contact with a person. However, the self-help oriented patron certainly exists, and ensuring that the academic library's web site organization serves that patron is also critical.

REFERENCES CITED

"Ask a Milner Librarian." 2002. <http://www.mlb.ilstu.edu/service/askmerl.htm>.

Buckland, Michael. 1987. "Combining Electronic Mail with Online Retrieval in a Library Context." *Information Technology and Libraries* 6, no. 4 (December): 266-271.

Bruman, Janet L. 1985. "Customizing Electronic Mail: User Programmed Online Forms and Online Instructions on OnTyme Electronic Mail." In *National Online Meeting, Proceedings* compiled by Martha E. Williams and Thomas H. Hogan, 57-69. Medford, NJ: Learned Information, Inc.

Carr, Margaret M. 1981. "Benefits and Pitfalls of Electronic Mail." In *National Online Meeting, Proceedings* compiled by Martha E. Williams and Thomas H. Hogan, 91-96. Medford, NJ: Learned Information, Inc.

Choate, Ray. 1985. "The Online Revolution and the Reference Desk: the Australian Experience." *Special Libraries* 76, no. 1: 24-30.

Coffman, Steve, and Susan McGlamery. 2000 "The Librarian and Mr. Jeeves." *American Libraries* 31 no 5 (May 2000): 66-69.

De Gennaro, Richard. 1987. *Libraries, Technology and the Information Marketplace.* Boston: G.K. Hall & Co.

Dewey, Patrick R. 1989. *E-mail for Libraries.* Westport, CT: Meckler Corporation.

"Dialog's DIALMAIL Electronic Mail Service and Other New Features Announced at ASIDIC Fall Meeting." 1985. *Database* 8, (December): 12.

Dunker, Elke. 2001. "World Wide Web." In *Encyclopedia of Computers and Computer History*, edited by Raul Rojas, 843-845. Chicago: Fitzroy Dearborn.

Eager, Virginia W. 1981. "Electronic Mail in the GTE Information Service." In *National Online Meeting, Proceedings* compiled by Martha E. Williams and Thomas H. Hogan, 179-181. Medford, NJ: Learned Information, Inc.

"Electronic Mail Systems Update." 1982. Library Systems Newsletter 2, no. 1 (January): 1-3.

"Electronic Mail Systems Update." 1984. *Library Systems Newsletter* 4, no. 4 (April): 30-32.

Greene, Araby. 2002. "Providing Electronic Reference Service." In *Attracting, Educating, and Serving Remote Users Through the Web* edited by Donnelyn Curtis, 73-116. New York: Neal-Schuman.

Gross, Melissa; Charles R. McClure; and R. David Lankes. 2001. Assessing Quality in Digital Reference Services: Overview of Key Literature on Digital Reference. Tallahassee, FL: Information Use Management and Policy Institute. Retrieved from <http://dlis.dos.state.fl.us/bld/Research_Office/VRDphaseII.LitReview.doc> on 4/14/2003.

Hauben, Michael. 2001. "ARPANET." In *Encyclopedia of Computers and Computer History* edited by Raul Rojas, 49-52. Chicago: Fitzroy Dearborn.

Hiltz, Starr Roxanne, and Murray Turoff. 1978. *The Network Nation: Human Communication via Computer.* London: Addison-Wesley.

Hoss, Eric, ed. 2002. *College Blue Book.* 29th ed. Vol. I, *Narrative Descriptions.* New York: MacMillan Reference USA.

Howard, Ellen L. and Terry Ann Jankowski. 1986. "Reference Services via Electronic Mail." *Bulletin of the Medical Library Association* 74, no. 1: 41-45.

Janes, Joseph. 2002. "Digital Reference: Librarians Experiences and Attitudes." *Journal of the American Society for Information Science and Technology* 57, no. 7: 549-566.

Janes, Joseph, Chrystie Hill, and Alex Rolfe. 2001. "Ask-an-Expert services analysis." *Journal of the American Society for Information Science and Technology* 52, no. 13 (November): 1106-1121.

Janes, Joseph David Carter, and Patricia Memmot. 1999. "Digital Reference Services in Academic Libraries." *Reference and User Services Quarterly* 39, no. 2 (winter): 145-150.

Josephine, Helen B. 1980. "Electronic Mail: the Future is Now." *Online* 53, no. 7 (October): 41-43.

Lankes, R. David and Abby S. Kasowitz. 1998. "The AskA Starter Kit: How to Build and Maintain Digital Reference Services." ERIC Clearinghouse on Information and Technology. Syracuse, NY. [BBB30993].

Lederer, Naomi. 2001. "E-mail Reference: Who, When, Where, and What is Asked." In *Evolution in Reference and Information Services: The Impact of the Internet* edited by Di Su, 55-73. New York: The Haworth Press, Inc.

Lee, Joel M. 1984. "ALANET: Building an Electronic Information Service." *Library Hi Tech* 2 no. 3: 63-68.

Robson, Gary. 2001. "Electronic Mail." In *Encyclopedia of Computers and Computer History* edited by Raul Rojas, 273-275. Chicago: Fitzroy Dearborn.

Schneider, Karen G. 2000. "My Patron Wrote Me a Letter: the Joy of E-mail Reference." *American Libraries* 31, no.1 (January): 96.

"Serving the Internet Public: The Internet Public Library." 1996. *Electronic Library* 14, no. 2 (April): 122-126.

Shields, Paul. 2001. "America Online." In *Encyclopedia of Computers and Computer History* edited by Raul Rojas, 25-26. Chicago: Fitzroy Dearborn.

Sleeth, Jim and James LaRue. 1983. "The ALL-OUT Library: a Design for Computer Powered Multidimensional Services." *American Libraries* 14, no. 9: 594-596.

Sloan, Bernard G. 1990. *Linked Systems for Resource Sharing.* Boston: G.K. Hall & Co.

Spencer, Donald D. 1997. *The Timetable of Computers.* Ormond Beach, FL: Camelot Publishing Co.

"The Use of Electronic Mail in Research Libraries." 1998. *SPEC Kit* no.149 (December).

Turlington, Shannon. 1999. *Field Guide to Colleges.* New York: MacMillan Reference.

Weise, Freida O. and Marilyn Borgendale. 1986. "EARS: Electronic Access to Reference Service." *Bulletin of the Medical Library Association* 74, no. 4: 300-304.

Whitaker, Becki. 1989. "Electronic Mail in the Library: A Perspective." *Library Trends* 37, no. 3 (winter): 357-65.

White, Marilyn Domas. 2001. "Diffusion of Innovation." *Journal of Academic Librarianship* 27, no. 3: 173-187.

Woodford, Chris. 2001. "Browser." In *Encyclopedia of Computers and Computer History* edited by Raul Rojas, 119-121. Chicago: Fitzroy Dearborn.

Woodford, Chris. 2001. "Yahoo!" In *Encyclopedia of Computers and Computer History* edited by Raul Rojas, 859-861. Chicago: Fitzroy Dearborn.

Zakon, Robert Hobbes. 2003. "Hobbes' Internet Timeline v6.0." <http://www.zakon.org/robert/internet/timeline/>.

The Internet Public Library
as a Teaching Tool
for Shockingly Traditional Reference Skills

Abigail Leah Plumb

SUMMARY. The Internet Public Library is an experimental educational initiative of the University of Michigan School of Information. The author, a Michigan alumna, argues that the Internet Public Library can play a role in the education of reference librarians, with particular attention to the traditional reference skills it fosters. She discusses her own experience with the IPL and QRC, its digital reference tool, as a library student, positing that the value of the IPL lies in the way it renders individual aspects of the reference process explicit and forces its users to examine them piece by piece. *[Article copies available for a fee from The Haworth Document Delivery Service: 1-800-HAWORTH. E-mail address: <docdelivery@haworthpress.com> Website: <http://www.HaworthPress.com> © 2004 by The Haworth Press, Inc. All rights reserved.]*

KEYWORDS. Internet Public Library, University of Michigan School of Information, digital reference, library school, reference, skills, virtual reference, e-mail

Abigail Leah Plumb is Librarian/Information Specialist, Lippincott Williams & Wilkins, a medical publisher.

Address correspondence to: Abigail Leah Plumb, 560 Riverside Drive, #8M, New York City, NY 10027 (E-mail: libronaut@yahoo.com).

[Haworth co-indexing entry note]: "The Internet Public Library as a Teaching Tool for Shockingly Traditional Reference Skills." Plumb, Abigail Leah. Co-published simultaneously in *The Reference Librarian* (The Haworth Information Press, an imprint of The Haworth Press, Inc.) No. 85, 2004, pp. 33-41; and: *Digital versus Non-Digital Reference: Ask a Librarian Online and Offline* (ed: Jessamyn West) The Haworth Information Press, an imprint of The Haworth Press, Inc., 2004, pp. 33-41. Single or multiple copies of this article are available for a fee from The Haworth Document Delivery Service [1-800-HAWORTH, 9:00 a.m. - 5:00 p.m. (EST). E-mail address: docdelivery@haworthpress.com].

http://www.haworthpress.com/web/REF
© 2004 by The Haworth Press, Inc. All rights reserved.
Digital Object Identifer: 10.1300/J120v41n85_03

I must confess that I wasn't entirely new to the idea of e-mail reference when I came to library school. In the mid 1990s, I interned for several summers at a business news organization in New York City (the company founder is now the mayor, if that narrows it down at all . . .). I learned early in my tenure there to take advantage of their library as much as possible: I would use the idiosyncratic messaging software on the company's proprietary network to request articles on a given topic, and received the documents within a day or two, via the same awkward text-messaging. I don't recall being interviewed at all about my particular needs; while I'd like to think that was a direct result of my nuanced and articulate reference requests, I'm sure that it had much more to do with the relative newness of the medium, as well as the awkwardness of the particular interface. Conducting a traditional reference interview in an asynchronous digital-text environment was not part of the average librarian's repertoire then; if it isn't yet, that's not for lack of trying by the University of Michigan School of Information (SI) and a few other library schools who are incorporating digital reference into their reference curricula.

Perhaps the business news librarians with whom I corresponded knew about the IPL; I certainly didn't, and wouldn't for several more years. But by the summer of 1997, the IPL was already flourishing, providing the public e-mail reference, virtual story hour and a number of other traditional library activities and tasks, transposed into digital media. When I made its acquaintance three years later, the IPL had an enormous number of dedicated reference volunteers, professional librarians and students of library schools across the country, as well as students at SI, the IPL's home institution. Its web site was sophisticated for the day, and its employees, volunteers and student workers were educated and enthusiastic about the project. The IPL was then–and remains today–an SI institution.

In my first semester at SI, I took Maurita Holland's reference class, which required answering questions for the IPL. For those of us who enjoyed working with computers as much as possible, computer-mediated reference seemed fun and novel, my previous experience notwithstanding. Despite its cutting-edge aura, though, the IPL gave us a chance to develop and hone the most traditional reference skills, such as understanding patrons' information needs, and responding to those needs appropriately. By slowing down the reference interaction, rendering each step more explicit and providing a record of exactly what we said and did, our IPL assignments let us examine our interactions with patrons and attempt to learn from our–and others'–mistakes.

Over the past five to ten years, e-mail reference has become common in libraries, but anecdotal evidence suggests that library schools have been slower in embracing the new medium. Perhaps developers of curricula feel that asynchronous digital reference requires no skills in addition to those developed for in-person reference; whether that is true is a topic for other papers. I propose an inverse perspective to this one with respect to the purpose and place of e-mail reference programs like the IPL in graduate library education: asynchronous digital reference, with its funhouse-mirror version of the traditional reference process, is an invaluable tool in teaching the traditional skills necessary for reference in any medium, and with any level of machine mediation.

A BRIEF HISTORY OF THE INTERNET PUBLIC LIBRARY

The Internet Public Library began as a class examining just what an "Internet Public Library" might be. Joseph Janes (1998), the originator of the Internet Public Library idea at Michigan, writes that "from the very beginning, the project was motivated by one central question: *What does librarianship have to say to the network environment and vice versa?*" Janes posited from the outset that the work of a brick-and-mortar library and that of an online library would be similar in some ways and very different in others, writing "I think we need to create an entity that people can recognize both as a library and as a 'true' Internet institution . . . the only thing I will insist on is a story hour, but how that might work I have no idea." The IPL has stayed remarkably true to Janes's vision.

As the IPL has evolved, it has retained recognizable library functions in addition to the successfully implemented story hour, including classification of resources, guides to research, and, of course, e-mail reference.[1] Today, it includes "Kidspace" and "Teenspace" sections, as well as "Ready Reference" and other collections; there is still a story hour, as well as a page called "Say Hello" including greetings in many languages. Most important to reference education is the e-mail reference program, in which volunteers from many different library schools, as well as a cadre of professional librarians, answer questions submitted via e-mail or through a web form.

As I write this, the future of the Internet Public Library is in doubt. Despite kudos from the library and educational communities, its seed money and grants have run out. Universities across the U.S. are tightening their belts, and among the casualties in Michigan are library and community outreach programs. The IPL is one of UM's endangered programs and unless its limited needs can be met, its continued service to the Internet community may be forced out of existence.

THE IPL IN SI's REFERENCE CURRICULUM

SI 647: Information Resources and Services is offered in the fall semester, which means that the newest library students at Michigan frequently take it; I was one of these students in the fall of 2000. Among our assignments was to answer one IPL question a week for six weeks. After we learned the policies of the IPL reference service, and got a crash course in using the QRC software, we chose from among the many unanswered questions and answered one per week. The tangible product of each week's assignment was a copy of the actual patron interaction along with a description of the student's logic at each step and a certain amount of postmortem self-evaluation in which we tried to address as many aspects of the interaction as possible. What was the question, and what did the asker want to know? Why did we start our search by looking in the places we did? Did we think we knew the answer when we started exploring? Did we stumble on the answer serendipitously or find it methodically? While we completed this task, we also worked on others, including a weekly sheet of questions we were intended to answer using a particular genre of resources, and the evaluation of a shelflist of reference works from Little Big Horn College, a tribal college in Montana. These tasks and our work at the IPL informed one another as we learned to address patrons' questions and evaluate reference resources.

Because the IPL reference interactions were asynchronous and text-based, we students had both the time and the inherent psychological distance of text in which to evaluate, modulate, and control each step of our reference interactions. We had the opportunity to learn, slowly and without the immediate (and potentially terrifying) presence of a patron, how to examine and evaluate a patron's question with care; how to figure out where to start searching; how to organize the information gleaned and how to respond to the patron in a comprehensible way. None of these tasks is specific to text-based or asynchronous reference; each one is necessary whether the interaction is mediated by e-mail chat software, whether it occurs over the telephone or over the top of the reference desk. But working for the IPL as students allowed us to develop these skills with actual patrons without exposing us, wet-behind-the-ears proto-librarians that we were, to the perils of an in-person interaction. We would already have experience once we were ready to face an actual patron in the flesh.

The written questions that filter through QRC give each student the opportunity to read their text as many times as he or she desires; over time, the members of my reference class became more attuned to the nuances of this particular mode of communication. To the newest students, this reading of the initiating e-mail can be a deliberate, iterative process: at the first read-through, the reader may gain only the specific piece of information the patron was requesting. The second time, the reader may absorb more facts about the patron, either from the text of the question or from the other information provided. (If the question has come in via e-mail, it may have nothing more than an e-mail address in addition to the text of the question, whereas if it has come through one of the web forms, patrons typically filled out most or all of the numerous form fields, such as physical location, the reason for the question, or the places the patron had already looked.) A third read-through may reveal article problems characteristic of a non-native speaker of English, or perhaps some misapprehension about the nature of the World Wide Web that the reference volunteer would need to set right in order to answer the question comprehensively. As we answered more questions, we slowly learned to glean this information from one or at most two read-throughs, simultaneously monitoring tone, style, unwitting disclosures by the patron as well as the expression of the information need itself. While many (probably most) reference interactions are initiated through means other than e-mail, and while many of us had already participated as paraprofessionals in reference interviews of sorts, these e-mail interactions gave us a chance to develop our ability to conduct the reference interview according to the information science frameworks we were learning. Later, when we had patrons coming to us in person, or calling us on the phone, as well as e-mailing us their questions, we were able to apply our new skills to absorbing and interpreting the additional information about a patron and her question contained in tone of voice, in posture, or through other means.

These e-mailed IPL questions arrived via a unique program called QRC ("quirk"), one of whose great strengths is collaboration. Michael McClennan developed QRC in the early days of the IPL to manage its questions and answers (Lagace, 1999). Using QRC, student volunteers have a unique opportunity to build a professional network, and to learn from the wisdom of those more seasoned. Everyone who works for the IPL, from the director to the newest of volunteers, can see one another's questions and any notes they have saved in the system. QRC may seem complicated to the very newest initiates, but once its users have answered a question or two with it, its advantages become clear to them. By its design, QRC deliberately allows volunteers to see how others have answered questions, and to request and offer help to one another; for brand-new reference students, the opportunity for informal collaboration was a valuable one. Many people, librarians and otherwise, know the feeling that a piece of information is *somewhere*, if only they can figure out where that place is. Experienced reference librarians learn to recognize instinctively whether a piece of information is likely to be recorded and accessible somewhere, but even the most experienced among us frequently rely on networks of colleagues to provide new perspectives when we're stumped. When a community of new searchers approaches questions in the QRC environment, they begin to develop and use such networks early, and they have the opportunity to rapidly develop their knowledge of necessary specific resources. They become good guessers quickly, and they learn to "ask around," in this case by posting a desperate plea for assistance or by flagging their question *need help* when in doubt. Sometimes the advice students receive contains the perfect resource, and sometimes it has more to do with when to let the question technically go unanswered, or when to point the asker to some LC subject headings, and call it a night. QRC provides an infrastructure that demonstrates to young librarians the value of cooperation with one another toward several different ends.

The IPL infrastructure also supports the cooperation between a question's asker and answerer–even when that collaboration feels more like an all-out brawl. One of the various flags with which a QRC user can mark a question is *ask info*; this means that she or he has queried the patron in order to get more information about a question. E-mail reference, particularly with QRC, renders this process formal and structured. IPL questions, partially because of the web form through which they're typically submitted, appear in diverse forms. One patron will produce a carefully-worded explanation of the thesis she's hoping to support with peer-reviewed journal articles, while another one will write, simply, "why I like school" in the space given. The need arises not infrequently for a volunteer to query a question's asker further. Is the latter patron a schoolchild trying to format a report on why he likes school, or is it an adult interested in the Keirsey Temperament Sorter? What kind of school is the patron curious about, and what kind of liking? How does the patron want to use the information? The slowness of formulating and sending these questions is a far cry from the casual "Okay, now, let me see if I have this right . . ." of an in-person reference interaction. This structure is an excellent way for student volunteers to cut their teeth on this interlocution, in that it forces them to return to the original question, evaluate what the gaps in their understanding are, and build a response to the patron that will eventually prove illuminating.

Once a given student had selected a few URLs, books or other resources, he or she is faced with the question, familiar to all reference librarians, of how to communicate this information to the original asker; one aspect of this problem is organization. Library students know—or learn quickly—that however useful Library of Congress Subject Headings may have been in locating those books about bees, those LC headings aren't going to be of much use to the fourth grader who asked the question about the bees in the first place. Nonetheless, it can be helpful to have a record of those LC headings while putting together an answer for the fourth grader. I learned, like many of my student colleagues, to take advantage of the "followup" function of QRC for this purpose. This allowed us to post notes, URLs, and draft responses—anything we might want to refer to later, but that wasn't yet ready for prime time. We could see how the various resources looked in plain text, and list them as we thought best; we could also play with different ways of arranging our answers before sending them out. We had the chance to play with organizing the components of our responses, to practice without having to generate them on the fly.

The final component of an IPL reference interaction, hard to separate from the issue of organization, is the production of an appropriate and comprehensible answer to the question. The IPL has strict guidelines as to what should be included in an answer, some related to content and some related to formatting. While there are few other reference situations in which the enclosure of a URL in pointy brackets is *verboten*, almost every reference situation requires the librarian to tailor her response to the needs of the patron. All of the IPL questions answered by volunteers must include certain features, including the answer or appropriate resources for further searching, and a description of what tools the librarian used to locate them. The guidelines urge volunteers to tailor their responses to the needs of the individual patron: "Try to determine the age and the English language comprehension level of the patron you are writing for. Try to find age-appropriate sources if the patron appears to be a child, and try to write in clear, short sentences if the patron appears to be having difficulty writing in English" (Internet Public Library). The IPL policy also states that volunteers should greet patrons by name when possible (and as appropriate), that they should mirror the question so as to make sure they understand what was asked; when wrapping up an answer, patrons are encouraged to reply if there's anything further they need to know, and are thanked for asking the IPL in the first place. While these guidelines are specific to the IPL and the e-mail reference process, they also highlight some important considerations for a new librarian–namely, how *do* you organize the information you're presenting to a patron, whether that patron is standing in front of you, waiting on the phone, or staring at an instant messenger window waiting for your response? The IPL guidelines suggest an answer up front ("According to the sources I consulted, the Pallas cat lives in Mongolia and throughout the Middle East") followed by an account of how that information was uncovered ("I started out by looking at the University of Michigan's Animal Diversity Web web site, located at . . ."). There's nothing magical about this particular structure, but the fact that the guidelines emphasize a structure at all, combined with the necessary act of typing the answer out and reading through it, forces a student to consider the organization and prioritization of an answer's many components–and gives that student the chance to see the sum total of what they've produced before it's dispatched to the patron, a rare luxury in a faster-paced or in-person environment.

Each of these different aspects of the Internet Public Library assignment forces UM library students to consider the reference process as a series of explicit steps, and therein lies its value. Few of us would consider it standard professional practice to keep a patron waiting while we stared into space, considering carefully the order in which we would reveal to them the articles we found; however, having had the luxury of this careful planning during the formative stages of our growth as librarians, we may instinctively apply what we've learned, even if we don't participate in an "Aska" or digital reference service ever again. While many of these activities may eventually be absorbed into the black box known as our expertise, the methodical collaborative business of learning reference at the IPL spotlights individual activities and processes that are vital to the development of a sturdy reference skill set. When examined from this perspective, digital reference reveals itself to be not only a faddish new extension of the traditional reference process, but an excellent teaching tool for developing creative, resourceful and adept reference librarians, and one that should not be allowed to slip away.

NOTE

1. Initially, the IPL staff wanted to incorporate real-time digital reference; while this was out of the question at the time, the IPL has experimented with this type of interaction, via MOO (a text-based, object-oriented multi-user environment). The MOO has not been part of my experience with the IPL; for more about the MOO, see Eustace, 2003; and Shaw, 1996.

REFERENCES

"Universities slash public outreach programs." *Detroit News*, Apr 23 2003.

Eustace, Ken. "Going my way? Beyond the Web and the MOO in the library: Internet Public Library and AussieMOO." *Australian Library Review*, 13 (1996): 44-53.

Internet Public Library. *Policy: Answering IPL Reference Questions*. 2003. web site. Available: http://www.ipl.org:2000/backroom/refvols/q-ans.pol.html.

Janes, Joseph. "The Internet Public Library: An Intellectual History." *Library Hi-Tech* 16.2 (1998): 55-68.

Lagace, Annette. "Our system is called QRC." *The Internet Public Library Handbook*. New York: Neal-Shuman Publishers, 1999. 158-9.

Shaw, Elizabeth. *Real-time Reference in a MOO*. 1996. web site. Available: http://ipl.sils.umich.edu/div/iplhost/moo.html.

"Contact Us":
Archivists and Remote Users
in the Digital Age

Katharine A. Salzmann

SUMMARY. Archive repository web pages have become more sophisticated in the past several years, and information about repository holdings is often readily available online. However, so long as full archival records are not available electronically, archivists will have to contend with the increase in reference requests from remote users. The author surveyed one hundred university archives web pages to examine the current availability of archival records on the Web and to explore the possible effects of this presence on archivists' efforts to provide remote users with access to repository holdings through "ask an archivist" forms, electronic mail, and other modes of communication. *[Article copies available for a fee from The Haworth Document Delivery Service: 1-800-HAWORTH. E-mail address: <docdelivery@haworthpress.com> Website: <http://www. HaworthPress.com>* © 2004 by The Haworth Press, Inc. All rights reserved.]

KEYWORDS. University archives, World Wide Web, electronic reference, virtual reference, archives and archivists, remote users

Katharine A. Salzmann is Archivist and Curator of Manuscripts, Morris Library's Special Collections Research Center, Southern Illinois University Carbondale, Carbondale, IL 62901.

[Haworth co-indexing entry note]: " 'Contact Us': Archivists and Remote Users in the Digital Age." Salzmann, Katharine A. Co-published simultaneously in *The Reference Librarian* (The Haworth Information Press, an imprint of The Haworth Press, Inc.) No. 85, 2004, pp. 43-50; and: *Digital versus Non-Digital Reference: Ask a Librarian Online and Offline* (ed: Jessamyn West) The Haworth Information Press, an imprint of The Haworth Press, Inc., 2004, pp. 43-50. Single or multiple copies of this article are available for a fee from The Haworth Document Delivery Service [1-800-HAWORTH, 9:00 a.m. - 5:00 p.m. (EST). E-mail address: docdelivery@haworthpress.com].

INTRODUCTION

Every semester, archivists in academic libraries conduct numerous "introduction to research in the archives" workshops for undergraduate and graduate classes at their institutions. In recent years, as the end of each session approaches, a student invariably raises his or her hand and asks whether anyone has ever thought of digitizing the archives' holdings and providing access to them online. In this age of instant Internet gratification, Google™ searches as a substitute for research, chat-messaging reference, personal scanners, and highly publicized digitization projects, an archivist might understand why a student would assume that digitizing the entire collection would be a possibility. While understandable, the question is still frustrating–especially after he or she has spent the previous fifty minutes trying to instill in the students the intricacies of research using primary sources.

University and college archive repositories' web interfaces have become much more sophisticated in the last decade, and they continue to evolve along with those of academic libraries, manuscript repositories, and state and federal government archives. Still, archives' web sites do not provide full, online access to the rich array of the repositories' holdings. The demand for complete access to archival records will continue to increase, however, especially as more and more repositories make their descriptive finding aids available on their web pages. Since electronic versions of university archives holdings are not wholly available on the World Wide Web, and are not likely to be in the near future, archivists must continue to serve as the intermediary between remote users and university records, and they must continue to manage increased demand for access through "ask-an-archivist" forms, electronic mail, and other forms of communication including modes perhaps not yet implemented or conceived.

CURRENT LITERATURE

A review of recent library literature reveals a wave of articles and monographs on the development of and trends in electronic, instant messaging, and/or synchronous reference service in academic libraries. In a 2002 article in *Internet References Services Quarterly*, Mohamed Taher examines the developing art of the web-based reference interview to determine its effectiveness in saving the interviewee's time. He finds that further research is necessary to answer this question, but is able to conclude that more libraries are migrating from e-mail reference to interactive reference models.[1] In *College and Research Libraries*, Marianne Foley reports on a case study conducted of the University of Buffalo's instant-messaging reference service in its university library. She concludes, "Chat reference will not supplant the library's other reference services, but it offers another way to reach and educate patrons."[2]

The unique nature of archival records, the fact that they are generally not available through interlibrary loan programs, and the archival profession's continued efforts to make information about their holdings more accessible all contribute to the development of archivists' use of electronic mail in answering reference queries from remote users. Although archivists have been conducting so-called "virtual reference interviews" at least as long, if not longer, than their colleagues at the reference desk in academic libraries, much less research exists on the topic. Wendy Duff and Catherine Johnson conducted a recent analysis of the types of reference questions archivists receive via electronic mail, and found that research questions fall into a number of categories, including: service requests, material-finding, user education, directional, fact-finding, and consultation.[3] Kristin E. Martin also examines various types of remote reference questions posed to academic archivists at the University of North Carolina at Chapel Hill and finds support for her hypothesis that "the types of questions asked by users have become more specific as more holdings information has become available through online catalogs and web pages."[4] In a 1995 article for *The American Archivist*, Helen Tibbo explores remote reference interviewing techniques and argues "It is not hard to envision entire archival and manuscript collections being available electronically one day," but that "right now that day is still well in the future."[5] In 1995, during the infancy of the World Wide Web, the possibility that everything could (and should) be digitized was perhaps more likely than it is today.

METHOD

This study will evaluate the current availability of archival records on the World Wide Web and explore the possible effects of this availability on archivists' efforts to provide remote users with access to repository holdings. The repositories examined in this study represent a sample of Association of Research Libraries (ARL) university and college archives. ARL university archives were chosen for a number of reasons, including the expectation of professional leadership from ARL institutions and the broad geographic representation across the United States and Canada. The deciding factor for choosing university archives as opposed to manuscript repositories, or special collections in general, is that each host university has only one university archives, while they might support a number of other repositories. Another influence in the choice of university archives was collecting scope. University archives encompass records of the host institution that contain enduring legal, financial, or historical value, and the deposit of records is often mandated by a state or institutional records management schedule. The types of records housed in various university archives are fairly uniform: record groups consist of materials created in the daily activities of university departments or organizations, preserved according to the university's records retention schedule; faculty papers that reflect the activities and accomplishments of university faculty members; university publications, including printed material such as reports, board of trustees minutes, course descriptions and yearbooks; and photographs documenting people, events, and places that have shaped the university and the broader community. These factors mean that, by nature, the records have a local geographic focus, but could attract remote researchers including academic scholars, local historians, graduate and undergraduate researchers, and alumni who relocated after graduation.

In order to evaluate the current availability of web-based archival records, the author surveyed one hundred ARL university archives web pages in March 2003. Each ARL member institution had a web page devoted to university archives, but the amount of information provided varied considerably. The web sites were evaluated on four points: (1) availability of complete descriptive finding aids for university archives record groups, (2) availability of the university archives' manuscript and/or published materials in digital form, (3) availability of the university archives' photograph holdings in digital form, and (4) whether, and by what means, the information on the web page directs the remote user to contact the university archivist for additional information. When conducting the evaluation, the author appreciated that web pages are evolving entities, and that both the migration of traditional paper finding aids to electronic documents and the digitization of records require concentrated amounts of time and labor. Therefore, credit was given if a repository had made significant progress toward either of these endeavors, and if the web page showed evidence that the current content was part of a continuing initiative.

RESULTS AND ANALYSIS

Web-based finding aids: The common access point for research with archival records is the descriptive inventory, or the finding aid. Finding aid formats vary among repositories, but some components of the document are universal: the creator sketch or record group history, provides a brief accounting of the person, organization, or department represented by the collection; the scope and content note should explain which records are in the collection; the series description outlines how the material within the collection is arranged; and the inventory, or container list, provides a listing of each box and folder of the collection. Each university archives' finding aid for a collection or record group might have none, one, two, or all of the first three components, but it must have the last, the container list, in order to be effective in providing access to the records.

For the purpose of this study, the author specified that the minimum requirement for an online finding aid would be a box and folder listing. This eliminated a number of repositories providing overviews of their university archives record groups that, while descriptive, did not inform users of the full content of the collections. Of the one hundred university archives web pages surveyed, forty-six (46%) provided finding aids for their record groups on their web sites. Twenty-nine (63%) of these forty-six used Hyper Text Markup Language (HTML) for their finding aids. Fourteen (30.5%) provided finding aids according to the latest standard in archival description, Encoded Archival Description (EAD), and three (6.5%) converted their paper finding aids through Portable Document Format (PDF) technology.

How does either the existence of, or the lack of, web-based finding aids affect archivists' interaction with their remote users? In 1992, the Society of American Archivists (SAA) published a seven-volume *Archival Fundamentals Series* "conceived and written to be a foundation for modern archival theory and practice."[6] In the volume dedicated to the history of and trends in archival reference services, Mary Jo Pugh argues that "users should have the freest possible access to finding aids in or near the reading room without staff intervention, since the purpose of finding aids is to make the user as free of the archivist as possible."[7] In recent years, repository web pages have become virtual extensions of their reading rooms, and having access to full inventories on the World Wide Web allows the remote researcher a certain level of autonomy in conducting research—similar to what on-site patrons enjoy in the physical reading room.

However important to the research process, finding aids are still only descriptions of the collections, and they are not substitutes for the records themselves or for the information contained within. The more finding aids an archivist provides electronically, the more remote users will request access to archival records. For repositories that have web pages without finding aids, archivists can also expect an increase in the number of requests from remote users, either for inventories or for further information about the holdings.

Availability of archival records: Historically, archivists have been at the forefront in providing information on the World Wide Web. Numerous academic libraries and archives have launched digital archives initiatives and scanning projects, resulting in an increased awareness of and access to archival records. To fulfill the second goal of this study, the web pages of each of the one hundred ARL university archives were assessed to determine whether or not they contained digital reproductions of university archival records, publications, and/or photograph materials.

Of the one hundred university archives web pages surveyed, many provided digitized records from the university archives, but a majority of these records were presented as part of online exhibits or subject guides and did not represent a clear initiative to provide remote users with full access to the university archives' holdings. Only seven (7%) of the web pages provided web-based archival collections and included a digital initiatives statement on the repository web page. Three of these initiatives were local, involving only the records of the university archives at the host institution. Three stemmed from university consortiums' efforts to provide access to digital representations of archival records from a number of repositories, and one project was in conjunction with its state digital library project.

Fourteen (14%) of the one hundred university archives web pages surveyed provided access to photograph holdings beyond images in online exhibits. Historically, visual records have been treated as an anomaly in university archives: they require different storage and handling conditions; different standards for arrangement and description; and more complicated copyright issues. As a result, archivists and patrons often overlook visual materials as sources of information. However, visual records lend themselves well to digital reproduction, and they are frequently the first items that archivists digitize and make accessible on the Web. This study found that twice as many repositories have initiatives to provide web-based access to their photograph collections than their text records.

Why are so few repositories currently providing access to their archival records on the World Wide Web? What does this mean for the remote user? Several theories explain the low number of digital initiatives in university archives. The sheer quantity of archival records is an obstacle. Repositories that have digital initiatives have attempted to overcome this by focusing on frequently accessed collections. Still, not everything can, will, or *should* be digitized in the near future, partly due to constraints caused by the volume of the material in question. The nature of university archival records can also contribute to issues of digitization. The institution's records retention schedule as well as confidentiality surrounding students, faculty, and personnel impact what archivists can make available on the World Wide Web. Another reason for the current lack of web-based archival resources is that digitization is often an additional responsibility for already understaffed and overworked university archives departments struggling to provide basic services. And finally, there are considerations concerning the process itself. Hardware, software, server space, and staff training all come with high price tags. In addition, the technology and universal standards for digitization are ever-changing. Until archivists can make significant strides in providing university archives in electronic form, remote users will have to rely on personal, individualized communication with university archivists for full access to the resources in the archives.

Contact us: For decades, archivists have provided "virtual" reference services to remote users by mail, telephone, facsimile and, since the late nineteen eighties, electronic mail. This survey confirms that archivists are well aware of their continuing role as intermediary between their patrons and the records entrusted to their care. Of the one hundred web pages surveyed, ninety-seven (97%) provided remote researchers with a means of directly contacting the archives staff. Forty-eight (49.5%) of these provided a general reference e-mail account, thirty-four (35%) provided a link to the university archivist's e-mail account, and fifteen (15.5%) provided a reference form accessible on the university archives web page.

CONCLUSION

Most university archives web pages provide remote users with general information about repository holdings and with a means of contacting the university archives staff for additional information. A handful of university archives have launched initiatives to provide their users with electronic versions of the repository holdings, but they are still in the initial stages. For the most part, actual content is lacking and remote users still need to rely heavily upon the archivist when conducting his or her research.

This survey aimed to assess the current availability of university archival materials on the World Wide Web. Archivists and other information professionals should conduct additional research on issues surrounding digitizing the full content of their archival collections. How are the current web-based collections being used? *Are* they being used, and by whom? Is digitization of a repository's entire holdings feasible? Would it be worthwhile? As archivists work to answer these questions, they must continue to keep in mind the needs of their users–both those of the patron who walks through the doors to the archives reading room, and those of the remote user who accesses the university archives web page from their home, office, library, or classroom.

REFERENCES

1. Mohamed Taher, "The Reference Interview Through Asynchronous E-Mail and Synchronous Interactive Reference: Does it Save the Time of the Interviewee?" *Internet Reference Services Quarterly*, 7, no. 3 (2002): 32.

2. Marianne Foley, "Instant-Messaging Reference in an Academic Library: A Case Study," *College and Research Libraries*, 63, no. 1 (January 2002): 45.

3. Wendy Duff and Catherine A. Johnson, "A Virtual Expression of Need: An Analysis of E-Mail Reference Questions," *American Archivist*, 64, no. 1 (Spring/Summer 2001): 49.

4. Kristin E. Martin, "Analysis of Remote Reference Correspondence at a Large Academic Manuscripts Collection," *American Archivist*, 64, no. 1 (Spring/Summer 2001): 38.

5. Helen Tibbo, "Interviewing Techniques for remote reference: Electronic Versus Traditional Environments," *American Archivist*, 58 (Summer 1995): 297.

6. Mary Jo Pugh, *Providing Reference Services for Archives and Manuscripts.* (Chicago: The Society of American Archivists, 1992): 1.

7. Pugh, *Providing Reference Services for Archives and Manuscripts*, 69.

Characteristics
of E-Mail Reference Services
in Selected Public Libraries,
Victoria, Australia

Doreen Sullivan

SUMMARY. An analysis of 96 question and answer pairs from the Bayside Library Ask a Librarian Service found that 54 percent of the queries were received from Bayside residents. Forty-seven percent of the e-mail reference questions were classed as research queries. Although only 25.1 percent of the queries were submitted for formal education purposes, all of these were research questions, and took longer than any other category to answer. In 2001, only 6 of the 54 questions submitted were tertiary level questions, but it took a median time of 95 minutes to answer each one. The 24 general interest category questions took a median time of 47.5 minutes to answer, which is almost half the time it took to answer a tertiary level query.

Librarians from three other public libraries in Victoria offering e-mail

---

Doreen Sullivan is Senior Reference Librarian, Bayside Library Service, Victoria, Australia.

Address correspondence to: Doreen Sullivan, 9/40 Ormond Road, Elwood VIC 3184, Australia (E-mail: kayaks5@bigpond.com).

This article is based on research conducted for a minor thesis for a Master of Business (Information Technology) at the Royal Melbourne Institute of Technology University.

[Haworth co-indexing entry note]: "Characteristics of E-Mail Reference Services in Selected Public Libraries, Victoria, Australia." Sullivan, Doreen. Co-published simultaneously in *The Reference Librarian* (The Haworth Information Press, an imprint of The Haworth Press, Inc.) No. 85, 2004, pp. 51-80; and: *Digital versus Non-Digital Reference: Ask a Librarian Online and Offline* (ed: Jessamyn West) The Haworth Information Press, an imprint of The Haworth Press, Inc., 2004, pp. 51-80. Single or multiple copies of this article are available for a fee from The Haworth Document Delivery Service [1-800-HAWORTH, 9:00 a.m. - 5:00 p.m. (EST). E-mail address: docdelivery@haworthpress.com].

Digital Object Identifer: 10.1300/J120v41n85_05

reference were interviewed, and compared and contrasted with the Bayside Library Service.

Issues of disproportionate labour, the appearance of the passive role of the e-mail reference user, and the wisdom of public libraries devoting significant resources to answer questions for formal education were raised. *[Article copies available for a fee from The Haworth Document Delivery Service: 1-800-HAWORTH. E-mail address: <docdelivery@haworthpress.com> Website: <http://www.HaworthPress.com> © 2004 by The Haworth Press, Inc. All rights reserved.]*

KEYWORDS. Ask a Librarian services, e-mail reference, public libraries, reference services, Bayside Library Service

E-mail reference services have existed since at least 1985.[1] Most of the literature on the topic, however, has focused on the academic or special library. Few studies have examined Ask a Librarian services in public libraries, yet public libraries are more likely to implement an e-mail reference service[2] over a chat or video-conferencing service.

Discussion of e-mail reference has waned and can be considered to be as quaint as discussion of telephone reference.[3] However, in February 2003 Sloan noted on the Dig_Ref list that a greater proportion of time was given to discussion of synchronous services such as chat than of asynchronous services such as e-mail reference. He suggested that e-mail reference still accounted for a large number of virtual reference queries, but suggested it was such a 'given' that it was rarely discussed.[4]

This paper investigates e-mail reference services in four public libraries in the state of Victoria, Australia, with particular emphasis on the Bayside Library Service. It especially examines whether research or ready reference questions are asked of the services, whether students are the main users of the services, whether public libraries will answer queries outside of their service communities, and to what extent individual public library services provide an answer in e-mail reference–if a full answer is provided or if sources and instruction to find answers are provided–and how the composition of these answers are packaged and presented.

BACKGROUND

When the author of this paper was given responsibility in the year 2000 for the Ask a Librarian e-mail reference service at the public

Bayside Library she found herself in an unfamiliar role. Although skilled in reference work and experienced in e-mail use, she was unsure if these two skills alone were sufficient to provide a quality e-mail reference service. In order to train herself she volunteered to answer questions at the Internet Public Library. The IPL is a digital library provided for the Internet community.

In May 2000, Victoria's Virtual Library (VVL) and its Ask a Librarian program was implemented.[5] Rostered staff members from public libraries in Victoria answer queries submitted to this site. Each month a different public library is responsible for the provision of answers, and so the responsibility is rotated among a number of different public libraries. Bayside Library Service participated in this program in May 2001 and October 2002. Several public libraries in Victoria have used the VVL as a training module prior to implementation of their own service.[6]

The author has participated in three e-mail reference services since 2000: the IPL, the VVL, and the Bayside Library Ask a Librarian service.

In her experience of answering questions received via e-mail at local, state and international level, the author has been at times startled at her perception that quite complex questions are asked and, given the level of research that these questions sometimes require, felt that some were inappropriate for public library services. In general, it was assumed by the researcher that the more complex a question was the more likely it would have been asked by someone who needed the answer for formal education.

She believed that a significant number of undergraduate level questions were asked of the Ask a Librarian service at Bayside. She noted postgraduate level questions of some complexity were on occasion posted to the IPL site. These questions included requests for literature reviews for master's level students. However, these questions may have been remembered because they appeared extraordinarily in-depth. She wondered if e-mail reference sites hosted by public libraries had students as their main users, or if the user range was broader. She wondered if Ask a Librarian services in public libraries served their own local community or if a wider range of people were served.

E-mail reference has been thought to suit quick, factual questions.[7-9] However, since 2000 onwards some researchers have considered e-mail reference to be suitable for research and complex questions.[10-14]

The IPL and the VVL are both virtual libraries with no physical building attached. Both are collaborative models where a number of people participate in reference provision on a rotation or volunteer basis. In individual public libraries however, one librarian alone often performs e-mail reference services.

Based on observation and experience of four separate Ask a Librarian services, questions arose about how public libraries offered their e-mail reference services. Were questions answered for anyone who asked them, regardless of where they were geographically based? Were tertiary students the main users of Ask a Librarian services? What was the nature of the questions asked? Were questions quick and factual or research based? How many questions were asked? How did librarians in public libraries answer these questions? How long did it take to research and compose an answer on average? Were e-mail answers presented and packaged, tailored for each individual? Does e-mail reference consume more time than in-person or telephone reference? How and why were e-mail reference services offered in public libraries? Was a greater service given to those who asked reference questions via e-mail instead of in person or on the telephone? Does the librarian do all the work and the question asker reap all the rewards? Does the user have a role in the reference process beyond submission of a question?

BAYSIDE LIBRARY SERVICE AND CITY BACKGROUND

Bayside Library Service is a metropolitan library service in Victoria that serves the suburbs of Beaumaris, Black Rock, Brighton, Brighton East, parts of Cheltenham, Hampton, parts of Highett, and Sandringham. It has a total population of 83,504[15] and 44.2% are registered library members.

Bayside City is considered an affluent area.[16] Over half (54.6%) of the households own computers.[17] Just over half (51.3%) used the Internet in the week preceding the 2001 census.[18]

Residents of Bayside tend to be highly educated, and work in 'white collar' professions, in particular business, education, and health.

The correlation between education, profession and e-mail reference use–those that are tertiary educated and are employed in education or information technology sectors are most likely to adapt to newer technologies[19-21]–appeared to be particularly apt for the population of Bayside.

PUBLIC LIBRARIES OF VICTORIA IN CONTEXT

Victoria is an interesting state to examine for e-mail reference services because:

1. it has at least one Internet access station in every library service;[22,23]
2. forty-one of forty-four public libraries subscribe to the Gulliver database consortium;[24]
3. 90.5% of Victorian public libraries have a web site,[25] and;
4. reference queries in Victoria have increased by 2.5% between the 1996/1997 and 2000/2001 financial years,[26] although many reference librarians in Victoria believe the increase is due to anomalies in the statistical collection process instead of an actual increase in queries.[27]

The Gulliver Consortium is a core collection of databases comprised of the Gale One File database, Gale Health & Wellness Center, and EBSCO ANZRC (Australian New Zealand Reference Centre) database.

The Australian Bureau of Statistics (ABS) indicated that public libraries in Victoria receive support from state and local government in the form of funds, grants, subsidies and materials, although each individual library is responsible for its provision of service.[28] State, National, virtual libraries (such as Victoria's Virtual Library), and commercial libraries were not examined here. In particular, the study sought to investigate if e-mail reference customers of the service area used the Ask a Librarian Service, or if customers from far beyond the service area–overseas or interstate–used it.

The Internet Public Library is not an actual public library under this definition (nor is it in Victoria). In fact, the Internet Public Library has experienced some financial difficulties over the years, precisely because it cannot tax its users. It now seeks corporate sponsorships.[29]

Both Bristow[30] and Gray[31] question the impetus behind offering e-mail reference services on a global scale, particularly when the funding for that service is provided for specific clientele at a local level. Mon[32] noted a propensity for people to contact government e-mail reference services such as her own Department of State Foreign Affairs Network (DOFSAN) for answers to questions that could be answered by local public or academic libraries. She used the example of a student who asked via e-mail where he could locate a copy of the standard reference work *Statistical Abstract.* She reported that government and other

Ask-an-Expert services were overwhelmed with queries, whereas libraries continued to report a low volume of questions received via e-mail. She suggested that because non-library digital reference services had no community tax or funding base to rely on, unlike traditional libraries, but provide free services to those who have not had their needs met at the local library, then local libraries should be invoiced for every question answered from their service community.

At the same time, whether it is in-person, telephone, or via asynchronous contact, students have always been users of public libraries and used the public library to assist with coursework.[33-35]

AIM OF STUDY

The aim of the investigation was to determine the type of questions asked of e-mail reference services in public libraries of Victoria, specifically whether the queries were ready-reference or research questions. The type of person who uses Ask a Librarian services based in public libraries could then be extrapolated.

From the broad aim above, a more specific series of objectives was established. These were to determine the type of questions received by e-mail reference services in public libraries of Victoria; how librarians composed and answered questions; and how an Ask a Librarian service fits within the overall reference section of the parent public library.

ANTICIPATED OUTCOMES

The researcher expected to find:

1. Most questions submitted to e-mail reference services in public libraries would be research questions.
2. Most queries submitted to Ask a Librarian services would be for formal education purposes.
3. Those students enrolled in formal education who use the service would be secondary and tertiary level students.
4. The volume of questions received by a public library e-mail reference service would be low.
5. The time taken by the librarian to answer questions would be significant. The librarian would probably take 50 to 60 minutes to research and compose an answer.

6. Users of e-mail and deferred reference services receive a higher quality of service than those within the library who undertake their own research.
7. The librarian would complete far more work in research of a question than the recipient would. This distribution of labour would be disproportionate. In traditional reference the user contributes more to the reference process.

REVIEW OF THE LITERATURE

Literature about e-mail reference has focused on models for digital service provision;[36,37] the digital reference interview or question negotiation;[38-40] analysis of questions asked and answers provided;[41-44] and the views and attitudes of librarians who offer digital reference services.[45,46]

Most e-mail reference services offered by libraries limit the service to their primary clientele and almost all services documented are services provided for the academic community.[47-52]

Literature that focuses on the public library (the Internet Public Library does not fit the criteria of a public library here) is primarily limited to the 2000 study by Garnsey and Powell. They found that of the e-mail queries they analyzed from 3 public libraries, 25 percent were classified as research queries. Another public library e-mail service contained in the literature is the 1999 overview of the e-mail reference service at the Santa Monica Public Library over ten years.[53] This piece, however, is more of an anecdotal and instructional practitioner paper.

Diamond and Pease,[54] in response to the studies by Garnsey and Powell and Gray, analyzed the digital reference service of a medium sized academic library at the California State University and found a digital reference service can answer the full range of questions asked. However, it was also found that complex or broad questions are more difficult to answer remotely. Thirty-five percent of questions received by the California State University were considered to be complex research questions.

Reference librarians reported a decline in the number of questions asked in general and in person at the reference desk,[55-57] but an increase in the complexity of questions asked.[58-61]

To find information the user would often turn to the Internet first before any other source,[62,63] although some users would differentiate between the library and the Internet, and choose the medium that best suited their information need.[64,65] Often there is a decided preference for

Internet use instead of library use.[66] This preference emerged as the clear preference of tertiary students born in the early 1980s.[67,68] Several reference practitioners and writers[69-73] suggested there is little need for library staff to assist people with quick, factual questions. Often the answers can be found on the Internet.

Although libraries and others are exploring real-time virtual reference in the form of chat and video, e-mail reference continues to be offered. For example, the National Library of Australia, all of the Australian State Libraries, and almost all Australian tertiary libraries offer e-mail reference.[74] The most common method for the submission of electronic reference questions is by e-mail.[75,76] Janes and Silverstein, reporting on an in-press study by Janes, found that within a two-year time frame the proportion of public libraries that offer e-mail reference has almost tripled. However, more academic libraries than public libraries provide e-mail reference.[77]

Volume of Queries

The volume of e-mail queries has been reported as low in previous years. Garnsey and Powell found in 2000 that the average number of queries received by public libraries in their study was 5.6 queries per week, and the most frequent response was 3 queries per week.[78]

In her overview of the Santa Monica Public Library e-mail reference service, O'Neill reported that in 1998 the library averaged ten reference questions by e-mail per month.[79] However, she contributed to discussion on the Dig_Ref list in February 2003 and estimated an average of 150 e-mail reference queries are now received per month, and most of these are responded to within 2 hours of receipt.[80]

Janes found that the volume of e-mail reference queries submitted to libraries varied between 4 and 208 per week.[81]

In comparison, non-library Ask an Expert services reported an overwhelming demand for e-mail reference. The Internet Public Library receives up to 1,000 questions per month.[82] In the year 2000 Ask ERIC received an average of 739 questions per week. In peak periods AskERIC receives up to 1,400 queries per week.[83]

Ability to Send Complex Documents in E-Mail Reference

In 1994 Tomer suggested that MIME compliant e-mail would enable messages to be exchanged so that complex documents could be included.

Imagine a user at the University of Washington sending the Institute for Jazz Studies at Rutgers University a request for information concerning Johnny Dodds, the clarinetist from New Orleans who played with Louis Armstrong and Jelly Roll Morton. In return, the user might receive a message from the reference librarian . . . that includes not only a text message about the conduct of the search, but also bitmaps of select pages of a relevant journal article, a digitized version of a photograph of Dodds, and a series of audio clips presenting representative musical selections as encapsulated segments of the message.[84]

Lankes found that intellectual products of reference, such as resource notes, could be shared with greater ease in the digital environment.[85]

Times of Day and Week to Ask E-Mail Reference Questions

Sloan[86] also found the most popular day of the week to ask a virtual question was Wednesday, as did Bushallow-Wilber et al.,[87] and so did McGlinchey[88] in her analysis of the questions asked of Victoria's Virtual Library July to December 2001.

Most people use e-mail reference on weekdays instead of the weekend. An e-mail reference service is likely to be used between the early morning hours of 12 a.m. and 6 a.m.

Users of E-Mail Reference Services

This section investigates both reported literature on whom the users are, and also examines services that accept queries from outside of their service communities. The majority of studies of e-mail reference focus on academic or specialist health or medical libraries, and therefore most of the information about users is about student users.

In the 1996 study by Bushallow-Wilber et al., of the university libraries of the State University of New York at Buffalo, graduate students used the service the most at 44 percent, followed by the faculty at 35 percent. Only 6 percent of undergraduates used the service.

Lederer, in her analysis of the e-mail reference service at the Colorado State University Library between August 1998 and May 2000 had 126 undergraduates pose questions, 141 graduate students and 179 non-CSU people post queries. She was disturbed by the 43 questions she classified as 'in-depth reference,' and noted a large number of people who asked these questions were 'non-affiliates asking questions that were not CSU-related.'[89]

As far back as 1988 providers of e-mail reference services were concerned with 'questions inappropriate to the service' such as the 'telephone number of the nearest authorized Sony repair dealer' sent to an academic library reference service.[90]

McGlinchey[91] in her report on Victoria's Virtual Library between July to December 2001, found the highest users of the service were from metropolitan Melbourne and the eastern suburbs (considered to be more affluent, educated, and established than other sections of Victoria) in particular. Fitzgerald and McGlinchey[92] found this to be the case in 2000, too.

McGlinchey also found the people who used the service the most were between 36-50 years old, and in general the questions asked were of a complex nature.[93] These questions were often also reaching Victoria's Virtual Library after the questioner had exhausted their own search skills.

In addition, she examined the nature of questions asked in relation to the age of the borrower. Of patrons aged thirteen years and under, 70 percent submitted homework questions; 75 percent of questions asked by those aged between 14-17 were research questions; and 50 percent of the questions asked by those aged between 18-25 were research questions, most often required for university study.[94]

Carter and Janes found that of the 3,000 questions they analyzed for the Internet Public Library 52 percent (1,073) of the questions were 'for a school assignment.'[95]

Scope of Services

Most academic libraries limit their service to students, faculty, and other affiliated users. Some public libraries limit their service to their community area, or questions about their community area, such as the Vancouver Public Library. The nearby Surrey Public Library limits its web-based services to cardholders only,[96] as does the New York Public Library.

The St. Paul Public Library, Minnesota, has answered queries from Italy, Germany, Seattle, and Los Angeles.[97]

Ten percent of the 178 queries submitted to Victoria's Virtual Library in its first year were from overseas, although this number had declined to 3.4 percent in 2001.[98]

In the year 2002 few of the 14 Ask a Librarian sites in Victorian public libraries listed (http://www.libraries.vic.gov.au) on the Victorian Virtual Library site had any limits placed on who may use their services.

Time Taken to Answer the Digital Reference Query

Reference work has almost always been time-consuming and labour intensive.[99,100] Janes[101] and Stover[102] noted that in general digital reference is more time consuming than traditional reference. Reported time to answer e-mail reference queries differs, but it ranges from 1 to 2 hours, reported by Jesudason in the examination of e-mail reference provided specifically for student athletes at the University of Wisconsin-Madison.[103]

Cunningham,[104] in writing about the New Zealand Digital Library for the Computer Science Community, noted that e-mail queries took up to an hour to construct a reply, which is far in excess of the 5-10 minutes of face-to-face reference transactions.

Botts[105] found that of twelve academic libraries that responded to her survey, the average time to answer an e-mail query was 49 minutes.

Discussion on the Dig_Ref Listserv in February 2003 compares the estimated time it took to complete a telephone reference query, an e-mail reference query and a chat reference query. Shalat reported that at the New York Public Library telephone queries took between 3-5 minutes to answer per call and e-mail reference queries took between 15-30 minutes to answer.[106]

Hegenbart (1998) examined the economics of the Internet Public Library. In assessing the reference section she found that on average it takes a person 40 minutes to answer the question and a further 10 minutes to type the answer.[107]

Even within 'historical' literature about e-mail reference as far back as 1992, practitioners noted the length of time it took to complete an e-mail query was in excess of that in traditional face-to-face reference.[108,109]

Expense of Digital Literature

Little has been written about the economics of virtual reference. Hegenbart discovered in 1998, with her analysis of the economics of the Internet Public Library, that the cost to answer each reference question was approximately $9.00.[110]

Some opinion pieces mention the expense of virtual reference, if not in clear economic terms, in terms of poor return on investment with the expenditure of staff effort for limited return.[111]

In an interview, Ann K. Symons, a library consultant in Alaska, noted that the newer virtual reference services are expensive, yet libraries are unwilling to drop any other services that are already in place.[112]

RESEARCH METHOD

The research method was formed after extensive reading of the literature, and is partially modeled on three studies: Garnsey and Powell;[113] Diamond and Pease;[114] and Powell and Bradigan.[115]

Diamond and Pease noted 'it is likely a more broader and diverse client base [than that of an academic library] would generate broader and more diverse questions.'[116]

Powell and Bradigan investigated who used the e-mail reference service at the John A. Prior Health Sciences Library at the Ohio State University, and categorized the questions asked. They found that due to the ease of technology customers who submitted an e-mail query received a greater quality and less costly service than those did that telephoned or came into the library.

This article built on these studies to investigate whether research questions are the most asked type of e-mail questions asked of Victorian e-mail reference services in public libraries. In an examination of questions a clearer picture emerged of the users of e-mail reference. This was determined by an examination of 96 Bayside Ask a Librarian service questions and answers between January 2001 and August 2002.

Through unobtrusive observation of content and transaction, and information supplied by the customer on submission forms and e-mail, a clear picture of the nature of questions asked at Bayside Library Service emerged.

A private (work) Microsoft Lotus Notes electronic archive folder (not available for public access) was maintained as part of the Ask a Librarian process.

Transaction analysis examined the time and date a query was submitted. Content analysis included demographic details, whether the query was ready-reference or research, and if the information sought by the user was for any of the following purposes:

- General
- Primary School
- Secondary School
- Tertiary Education
- Business.

The quantitative data collated from the unobtrusive analysis of the e-mail and deferred enquiries for Bayside were entered into Microsoft Excel spreadsheets, and formulas were used to calculate totals, medians, and percentages.

An overview of three other e-mail reference services in Victorian public libraries was investigated through a series of standardized open ended interviews of forty-five minutes duration to examine commonalties and differences and to establish whether a pattern arose from the responses.

The librarians were interviewed at a mutually convenient time for forty-five minutes about

- the implementation and history of their service;
- their philosophy and policy in answering e-mail questions;
- the training of librarians in the provision of the service;
- how the e-mails are composed and utilized (whether or not web links, audio files, etc., are used where appropriate); and copyright and database license issues.

The librarians were also asked for their perceptions on their service–how important it appears within their organization–and if a greater effort was put forth on behalf of the e-mail user, and attitudes librarians may have toward their customers in the provision of this service.

Of the forty-four public library services in Victoria, fourteen were found to offer e-mail reference. This was determined in by visiting the Victoria's Virtual Library site (http://www.libraries.vic.gov.au) on June 1, 2002. All public libraries in Victoria with a web site are registered here. By visiting each library web site fourteen e-mail reference services were found. The researcher searched for named links such as 'Ask a Librarian,' 'Electronic Reference Desk,' or 'E-Query.'

A purposive sample of e-mail reference services was chosen. All of the libraries had at least four branches to serve their population. Regional Library A serves a population of 388,263, of which 48.5% are library members.

Regional Library B serves a population of 220,745 and 45.2% of its population are registered library members. It was included because it was the first public library to implement an e-mail reference service in Victoria.

Suburban Library C was selected on the false assumption that it was the only Victorian library to have a 'dedicated' Internet Librarian, where the reference librarian is based in a 'back-room' role and does not have direct face-to-face contact with patrons, but works solely with responsibilities such as e-mail reference and construction and maintenance of the library web page.

Suburban Library C has a population of 305,206 and 60.1% are registered library members. Suburban Library C has the second highest use of the Gulliver databases.

Five library services were sent letters in October 2002 requesting an interview with the E-mail Reference Librarian(s). Four libraries responded. Three were able to participate.

DATA ANALYSIS AND RESULTS

Almost half (47.9%) of the 96 questions submitted to the Bayside Library e-mail reference were classified as research questions. In 2001, 58.5 ($n = 31$) percent of the queries were research questions. The average time to answer an e-mail query at Bayside was 64.5 minutes.

Although the *volume* of student questions received for both the e-mail and deferred reference queries was comparatively low, comprising an approximate twenty-five percent of all questions submitted, the *time* it took to find an answer per average query for this type of question was significantly longer than for any other type of category. Those enrolled in secondary education asked most student level questions of the Bayside Library Ask a Librarian Service.

All of the student level questions were classified as research questions.

The other public libraries reported a high use of their service by those needing information for primary school or lower secondary level.

Regional Library A reported receiving more research questions than ready-reference queries, and took an estimated average time of 15 minutes to answer e-mail reference. Regional Library B, however, reported receiving more ready-reference questions than research queries, and took an estimated average time of 60 minutes to answer e-mail reference queries.

Fifty-four percent (*n* = 52) of questions submitted to the Bayside e-mail reference service were asked by people resident in Bayside.

The most popular day to ask a query of the Bayside Ask a Librarian service was Tuesday, and the most popular month to submit a query was March.

All the libraries except one would answer queries outside of their service community, including queries from interstate or overseas.

Staff members at Bayside Library Service and Regional Library C were most likely to fully utilize all Internet functions such as links to articles within databases for authenticated users, and more prepared to type in material to answer a question if necessary.

The staff member at Bayside Library Service was the most likely to include individually constructed InfoMarks™ for the e-mail recipient.

Bayside Library Service was the only service to provide full answers to questions. The other libraries preferred to provide sources and some instruction.

Ready Reference and Research Questions for E-Mail Reference

Almost half of the questions submitted to the Bayside Ask a Librarian service were classified as Research Questions. In 2001 a greater proportion of research questions (58.5%) were submitted than ready-reference questions.

Volume of Questions Received, Time Taken to Answer

The Bayside Library Ask a Librarian service received 96 reference questions between January 2001 and August 2002. The total for 2001 was 53 and the total for 2002 was 46 (see Table 1).

The average number of queries received per week in 2001 was 1, and for 2002 it was 1.2 queries. The average number of queries received per month in 2002 was 4.4, and an average of 4.7 for 2001.

TABLE 1. Number of Ready Reference and Research Questions for Bayside E-Mail Reference

Year	*N*	%	Year	*N*	%	*N*	%
2001			2002			TOTAL	
Ready Reference	22	41.5%	Ready Reference	28	65.1%	50	52%
Research Question	31	58.5%	Research Question	15	34.9%	46	47.9%

The rounded average time to answer an e-mail reference query in 2001 was 79 minutes, and in 2002 it was 50 minutes. The average time to answer a query for both years is 64.5 minutes. Because averages are not necessarily representative, however, given that very high and very low results can skew the average, the median time it took to answer queries was also calculated. In 2001 the median time to complete an answer was 60 minutes. In 2002 it was 35.

Regional Library A reported an average of 15 minutes to complete questions. Regional Library B reported an average of 60 minutes to complete questions. Regional Library C preferred not to 'hazard a guess' because the time taken to complete an answer was dependent on what was asked.

Volume of Questions Asked by User Categories

Questions for the e-mail reference were categorized as general, business, primary, secondary, and tertiary. Questions asked for general information were the greatest category, which is not unexpected for a public library. Of interest, however, is in the year 2001 the second highest reason category people used the Ask a Librarian service was for business purposes (see Table 2).

The number of student questions asked was proportionately small compared to business and general question categories for the Ask a Librarian queries in 2001. The exception was the 2002 Ask a Librarian service where the second largest user category were students at 37.2% ($n = 16$). However, the *time* it took to answer the queries for formal education was significantly greater than the time it took to complete an answer for any other category. For example, between 2001 and 2002 only 12 (of 96) questions at tertiary level were asked of the e-mail reference service, but these questions took 21.5% of the documented time to answer. Overall time for all categories was entered as 6,393 minutes–106 hours, and 55 minutes (see Table 3).

TABLE 2. Volume of Questions for Ask a Librarian by User Category

2001	N	%	2002	N	%	TOTAL	N	%
Primary	0	0%	Primary	1	2.3%	Primary	1	1%
Secondary	4	7.5%	Secondary	9	20.9%	Secondary	13	13.5%
Tertiary	6	11.3%	Tertiary	6	14%	Tertiary	12	12.5%
Business	18	34%	Business	6	14%	Business	24	25%
General	24	45.3%	General	22	51.2%	General	46	48%

In comparison, twice as many business category questions (24) as tertiary level questions (12) were submitted, but took 25% of the overall time recorded to answer.

The median times it took to answer a question in each category, year by year, was also calculated. In 2001 it took 4,249 minutes–or 71 hours–to answer the total 53 Ask a Librarian questions. In 2002 it took 2,144–or 36 hours–to answer 43 Ask a Librarian questions (see Table 4).

Most Popular Days, Time of Day, and Months to Ask a Question

Those who used the Bayside Ask a Librarian service in 2001 asked the most questions on a Monday ($n = 14$). In 2002 it was Tuesday ($n = 12$). The most popular day overall was Tuesday ($n = 23$).

The least popular days in 2001 to submit questions were Saturday and Sunday, with 4 questions submitted on each day. Interestingly, in 2002, 8 questions were submitted on a Sunday which made it the second equal (along with Thursday) most popular day to ask a question. The ex-

TABLE 3. Proportion of Time Taken to Answer Each Category Question, E-Mail Reference

Category	N of Questions	Total Time in Minutes	Proportion Overall %
Primary	1	35	0.5%
Secondary	15	1088	17%
Tertiary	12	1378	21.5%
Business	24	1606	25%
General	46	2286	36%

TABLE 4. Median Time to Answer Questions by Category Type

	N of Questions	Median Time in Minutes	Proportionate Time %
2001			
Primary	0	0	0%
Secondary	6	60	10.5%
Tertiary	6	95	22%
Business	18	35	35%
General	24	47.5	32.5%
2002			
Primary	1	35	2%
Secondary	9	70	30%
Tertiary	6	47.5	21%
Business	6	20	5%
General	22	25	42%

perience of most services is that only a small volume of questions is received on the weekend.

In 2002 the least popular days to submit questions have been Friday and Saturday with 2 questions submitted on each day.

In 2001 August was the most popular month to ask questions, with 11 queries received, followed by March with 9 questions. In 2002 this pattern reversed with March the most popular month ($n = 10$) to submit a query, followed by August ($n = 8$). The most popular month overall was March, with 19 questions submitted, but it very closely followed by August with 18 questions. Although March could be considered the start of the tertiary academic year, the questions do not necessarily correlate to any school year or pattern.

Time of the Day

In accordance with the literature, most questions are asked when the library is open. However, in 2002 a greater number of questions were submitted in the evening, so it is possible this trend is changing. Conclusions cannot be drawn with such a small sample. The day was examined in fourths: 12:01 a.m. through to 6 a.m.; 6:01 a.m. through to midday; 12:01p.m. through to 6 p.m.; and 6:01 p.m. through to midnight (see Table 5).

These findings are very similar to most e-mail reference services reported in the literature, where questions are submitted during the day when the library is most probably open; the highest volume of questions tend to be received mid-week; and the least popular time to submit a question is the weekend, defined as Friday, Saturday, and Sunday.

Bayside Resident or Otherwise

Just over half–54 percent–of users of the Ask a Librarian service are residents in Bayside. Some are not residents and a significant proportion

TABLE 5. Most Popular Time Period to Least Popular Time Period to Submit a Query

2001	N	%	2002	N	%
12:01-6 p.m.	32	60.4%	12:01-6 p.m.	20	44.2%
6:01 a.m.-midday	15	28.3%	6:01 p.m.-midnight	11	25.6%
6:01 p.m.-midnight	4	7.5%	6:01 a.m.-midday	10	23.3%
12:01 a.m.-6:00 a.m.	2	3.8%	12:01 a.m.-6:01 a.m.	2	4.7%

is unknown (see Table 6). Public libraries do not have primary clientele in the same manner as a school or academic library. Bayside is prepared at the moment to answer queries from non-members or residents, and has answered queries from Paris, Florida, Seattle, and Queensland.

Regional Library A reported answering questions from Canada, India, France, and Perth.

Local Councils and the state government fund public libraries in Victoria. Most public libraries do not limit their service to their local community or to library members. While this is feasible for those libraries that receive a small volume of queries it is questionable whether it is fair to local residents and library members if the proportion of questions received from outside the service area is significant. The rationale behind this extension of service is in part to showcase and promote this kind of digital reference. However, e-mail reference is a relatively established function of reference now.

Regional Library B was purposively interviewed because a rumour surrounded its implementation of its Ask a Librarian service. Libraries that had participated in the pilot program of the VVL in 2001 heard from a representative of Library B that when the library first launched their e-mail reference service they were inundated with queries from around the world. In response Regional Library B limits its service to either questions *about* its service community or *from* its service community.

RESULTS FROM INTERVIEWS WITH RESPONDENTS FROM THREE OTHER LIBRARY SERVICES

Respondents from three regional library services that offer e-mail reference in public libraries of Victoria were interviewed to assess if Bayside Library was typical of Ask a Librarian services. They were also interviewed to gain an overall picture of how e-mail reference is delivered by public libraries in Victoria.

TABLE 6. Number of Questions Asked by Bayside Residents, Non-Residents, and Unknown for E-Mail Reference

2001	N		2002	N		TOTAL	%
Bayside Resident	27	50.9%	Bayside Resident	25	58.1%	52	54%
Non-Resident	14	26.4%	Non-Resident	8	18.6%	22	23%
Unknown	18	34%	Unknown	10	23.3%	28	33%

Fourteen of 44 public library services in Victoria appear to offer e-mail reference. Interviewing three representatives of three different library services represents 21.5 percent of those who offer it. If Bayside Library Service is included in this analysis the percentage rises to 28.6 percent. Although still a small sample, it reflected some general trends in the provision of e-mail reference in public libraries of Victoria.

All of the libraries had a common approximate launch date of 1999, and all were implemented as an extension of the reference service soon after the library web page was constructed.

Commonalties Between the Public Library
Ask A Librarian Services

Each respondent was based at library headquarters. Each library was modeled on a centralized reference service where the person based at headquarters would be responsible for the Ask a Librarian Service, the deferred enquiries for the entire library service, and each had a high degree of either expertise or technical support that allowed them to change and adapt the Ask a Librarian section of the web page as they saw appropriate.

These three services also emphasized the conservative model of reference where mostly sources were supplied in response to a question. The full answer was not. Given the large volume of questions received by two of these libraries it is not surprising sources are used to answer a question.

On their question submission form or web page these three libraries also indicated that queries of a factual nature would be answered by their service. Bayside Library does not have this policy, which may explain some of the complex questions received.

All of the libraries had a policy, stated or unstated, not to answer 'extensive' research questions, although none had a stated definition of what constituted 'extensive' research. The respondent at Regional Library A noted she will not 'trace' people and that such a request would constitute stalking.

Volume of Queries Received by Other
E-Mail Reference Services and Promotion

Bayside Library Service and Regional Library B both have their Ask a Librarian service placed in a less prominent position on the library web page than Regional Library A and Regional Library C.

Bayside Library and Regional Library B average an approximate four queries per month, and spend an approximate average of 60 minutes to research and compose an answer. Both libraries have an implied emphasis on presentation and packaging information.

Both A and C receive a surprisingly large volume of questions each month. Regional Library A estimated a rate of 30-40 questions submitted per month; Regional Library C suggested a volume of 60-75 queries submitted per month. Regional Library A received 200 questions in the 2001/2002 financial year.

Both A and C have their Ask a Librarian service placed very prominently on the web page. It is placed on every library web page, including the catalogue.

All of the libraries investigated, and this includes Bayside Library, rarely sent an e-mail to a customer to clarify a question. Bayside Library, Regional Library A and Regional Library C were more likely to telephone a customer if their information needs were unclear.

All libraries except Bayside provided sources to answer questions. Bayside Library provided a full answer to a question asked. Libraries A, B and C mentioned that sources were given because the user would probably have a clearer idea of what was needed, and if a broad source was provided, the user could narrow their focus. All expressed the belief that people often do not quite know what they are looking for, and even if they do, may be reluctant to share that information with the librarian.

Despite the above perception it was rare for any of the libraries to engage a user in a reference interview.

E-Mail Composition

Bayside Library Service was the most prepared to incorporate a number of presentation methods in an e-mail in response to a digital reference query. This service was most likely to design personal InfoMarks™ for a single user and place it in an e-mail. An InfoMark™ is a persistent uniform resource locator (URL) or link found in Gale Thompson InfoTrac™ databases. Two of the four core Gulliver databases are InfoTrac™ databases: the Health & Wellness Center, and OneFile.

Regional Library C was the next most likely respondent to use InfoMarks™, but preferred to link to perhaps one article only. Regional Library C saw InfoMarks™ as a promotional tool, and would limit use to 'teasers' to indicate to the user that much more was available in the Gulliver databases.

All libraries inserted web links–it was a 'given' for e-mail reference–but libraries A and B were unable to insert links to specific items in their catalogue. Bayside and C would insert links to specific items in their catalogue.

Libraries A, B, and C preferred to direct users to the Gulliver databases rather than search on the patron's behalf. Again, this was mostly explained as choice for the user. By serendipity or design, the user, searching the database, may find relevant information the librarian may not have thought to include.

The librarian at Bayside performs mediated searches on behalf of the patron. On reflection, this is unusual for a public library and is perhaps better suited to a corporate environment.

Nor is the mediated search at Bayside Library a patron-driven request, although patrons appear to appreciate the service. Overall 19 (20%, $n = 96$) unsolicited thank you e-mails have been received, from which a quality service can be inferred.

The difference in e-mail composition between Bayside Library Service and the other three libraries demonstrated each library service's approach to reference.

Libraries A and B adhered toward a conservative philosophy of reference, where a more instructive approach is given. Library C did not have an instructive approach, but provided source material for the answer, rather than a full answer. Bayside Library Service had a more liberal reference approach. Richardson et al.[117] asserted e-mail reference does not exist in a void alone, but that it must be incorporated into the overall reference policy and approach of its parent library.

Training of Librarians in E-Mail Reference Provision

All librarians learned about e-mail reference 'on the job' or trained themselves and refined their skills further 'on the job.' None had any formal training, and participation in the VVL came after their own e-mail reference service was established.

Personal Likes and Dislikes of E-Mail Reference

Interviewees were asked what they particularly liked and disliked about e-mail reference, and some common patterns emerged.

The common positive themes were: (1) the extension of the library service to 24 hours a day; (2) the ability to reflect upon the question asked and therefore the pressure for an immediate response is alleviated; (3) the challenge of answering the questions and determining what the user requires.

The common negative theme was the provision of incorrect information or insufficient detail by the customer, in particular contact details.

DISCUSSION OF ISSUES

. The issues that arose from this study focus on the philosophy of reference, and explored themes that have been discussed for at least a decade in the library profession.

In particular the issue of the imbalance of labour inherent in the liberal philosophy of reference is explored. Katz[118] asserted,

> Unfortunately, technology in the reference section has reinforced the Puritan notion that people must sweat to find answers.

When Katz wrote this line he may not have meant that the librarian must sweat on behalf of the customer instead. He continued,

> The librarian should be a true mediator between the individual and the frightening amount of information out there. In most cases this means coming up with the answers no matter how simple or complex or time consuming.

While this theory resonates in principle, the practice of public libraries providing e-mail reference for research questions is somewhat questionable. The invisibility of process–the customer does not realize the effort involved in finding an answer to some research questions–must undervalue the reference process itself and librarians. The customer, by asking an e-mail reference question (of any mediated-service), may not realize the difficulty of the request asked. However, there is some anecdotal evidence that users turn to library-based e-mail reference when they have exhausted their resources or been unsuccessful with Internet searches.

The State Library of Victoria, a public *research* library, has a policy to forward the user to their fee-based information service if the reference librarians have not been able to find an answer to a question within two hours.[119,120]

If an e-mail reference service is particularly custom-based, as it is at Bayside at the moment, and if it involves a large amount of time to find an answer to a question, which it quite often does, it may be desirable to move to a fee-based system for specific, involved research questions. Alternatively, the level of service that is currently offered may need to be reduced. The librarian has offered this level of service; it has not been a customer-driven introduction.

Another issue that appears prominent is the apparent number of one-person run e-mail reference services, combined with increased use of digital reference. Although librarians have always had specialization in some areas–corporate librarians, or business librarians, for example– it is possible that if e-mail reference librarians do not assess their service and plan for succession or at least for support, these librarians may very well burn out.

The implementation of the e-mail reference services in the libraries represented appears to be ad hoc, and not planned for the long term. E-mail reference is simply reference work presented in another medium, but somehow greater responsibility for the service falls to a sole person.

The last main concern is the perception that the user is divested of responsibility in the research process; the user seems to have a very passive role, but one in which the rewards may be great. Somehow it appears that the user has almost disappeared from the reference process. Do users have a role beyond submission of a question? Is their new role to evaluate material that people have worked on for them? Is the role of the reference librarian to produce intellectual content on an individual basis? This article has not answered the question of the role of the user, but it suggests it as a topic for further research, along with the division of labour and economic analysis of e-mail reference services.

REFERENCES

1. Howard, E. & Janowski, T. (1986). 'Reference services via electronic mail.' *Bulletin of the Medical Library Association*, 74, 300-304.

2. Janes, J. & Silverstein, J. (2003). 'Question negotiation and the technological environment.' *D-Lib Magazine*, 9(2). Available electronically from <http://www.dlib.org/dlib/february03/02contents.html>. Accessed 28 February, 2003.

3. Ryan, S. (1996). 'Reference service for the Internet community: a case study of the Internet Public Library Reference Division.' *Library & Information Science Research*, 18, 241-259.

4. Sloan, B. (2003). _[DIG_REF] E-mail reference: alive and kicking_ Yahoo! Groups. dig_ref. Digital Reference Services. February 20, 9:27 p.m. Available electronically from <http://groups.yahoo.com/group/dig_ref/post.html>. Accessed March 3, 2003.

5. Fitzgerald, B. & McGlinchey, S. (2001). 'What's overseas from the Internet: findings of the Victorian public library collaborative online reference project.' ALIA Public Libraries National Conference, 15 November. Available electronically from: <http://www.libraries.vic.gov.au/infonet/lol.htm#reports>. Accessed June 27, 2002.

6. *Ibid*, p. 13.

7. Lederer, N. (2001). 'E-mail reference: who, when, where, and what is asked.' *The Reference Librarian*, 74, 55-73.

8. O'Neill, N. (1999). 'E-mail reference service in the public library: a virtual necessity.' *Public Libraries*, September/October.

9. Straw, J.E. (2000). 'A virtual understanding: the reference interview and question negotiation in the digital age.' *Reference & User Services Quarterly*, 39(4), 376-379.

10. Diamond, W. & Pease, B. (2001). 'Digital reference: a case study of question types in an academic library.' *Reference Services Review*, 29(3), 210-218.

11. Garnsey, B.A. & Powell, R.R. (2000). 'Electronic mail services in the public library.' *Reference & User Services Quarterly*, 39(3), 245-54.

12. Gray, S.M. (2000). 'Virtual reference services: directions and agendas.' *Reference & User Services Quarterly*, 39(4), 365-375.

13. Janes, J. (2002). 'Digital reference: reference librarians' experiences and attitudes.' *Journal of the American Society for Information Science and Technology*, 53(7), 549-566.

14. Janes, J., Hill, C., & Rolfe, A. (2001). 'Ask-an-expert services analysis.' *Journal of the American Society for Information Science and Technology*, 52(13), 1106-1121.

15. i.d. Consulting, (2003). 'Bayside City Council community profile: 2001 and 1996 census information for the City of Bayside,' 4. Available electronically from <http://www.id.com.au/bayside/commprofile>. Accessed February 16, 2003.

16. *Ibid*, p. 16.

17. *Ibid*, pp. 31, 33.

18. *Ibid*.

19. Garnsey, B.A. & Powell, R.R. (2000). *Ibid*, p. 49.

20. National Office of the Information Economy. (2002). *The Current State of Play: Australia's Scorecard*. Canberra: National Office for the Information Economy, 8. Available electronically from <http://www.noie.gov.au>. Accessed May 4, 2002.

21. Missingham, R. (2001). 'Customer services in the National Library of Australia: leading edge or dragging the chain?' *The Australian Library Journal*, May, 151.

22. Fitzgerald, B. & McGlinchey, S. (2001). *Ibid*, 4.

23. Fitzgcrald, B. & Savage, F. (2002). 'From aardvark to xylophone: to bandwith from telephone.'

24. *Ibid*, p. 621.

25. Australian Bureau of Statistics. (2001). *Public Libraries 1999-2000.* Canberra: ABS, p. 4.

26. Local Government Division, Department of Infrastructure. (2002). *Annual Survey of Victorian Public Libraries.* Melbourne: Local Government Division, p. 18.

27. Murray Consulting & Training. (2003). *Review of the VISioN Reference Service: Final Report,* Ocean Grove: Murray Consulting & Training. Available electronically from <http://www.libraries.vic.gov.au/downloads/Library_Network_Unit/visionreviewfinal_ reportrev97>. pdf Accessed February 28, 2003.

28. Australian Bureau of Statistics. (2001). *Ibid,* p. 4.

29. Oder, N. (2003). 'Internet PL faces money crunch; How to support a "public good"? UMichigan to seek sponsors.' *Library Journal,* April 15, p. 17.

30. Bristow, A. (1992). 'Academic reference service over electronic mail.' *College & Research Libraries News,* 53, 631-637.

31. Gray, S.M. (2000). 'Virtual reference services: directions and agendas.' *Reference & User Services Quarterly,* 39(4), 365-375.

32. Mon, L. (2000). 'Digital reference service.' *Government Information Quarterly,* 17 (3), 309-318, p. 313.

33. Grosser, K. (1987). *Tertiary Students and Library Usage with Particular Emphasis on Public Libraries. A Report of a 1986 Melbourne Survey.* Melbourne: RMIT, Department of Information Services.

34. Gross, M. & Saxton, M.L. (2002). 'Integrating the imposed query into the evaluation of a reference service: A dichotomous analysis of user ratings.' *Library & Information Science Research,* 24, 251-263.

35. Haas, Warren J. (1962). 'Student use of New York's libraries.' *Library Trends* 10, 529-540.

36. McClennen, M. & Memmot, P. (2001). 'Roles in digital reference.' *Information Technology and Libraries,* September, 143-148.

37. Sloan, B. (1998). 'Service perspectives for the digital library: remote reference services.' *Library Trends,* 47(1), 117-143.

38. Abels, E.G. (1996). 'The e-mail reference interview.' *RQ,* 35(3), 345-359.

39. Janes, J. & Silverstein, J. (2003). 'Question negotiation and the technological environment.' *D-Lib Magazine,* 9(2). Available electronically from <http://www.dlib.org/ dlib/february03/02contents.html>. Accessed 28 February, 2003.

40. Straw, J.E. (2000). 'A virtual understanding: the reference interview and question negotiation in the digital age.' *Reference & User Services Quarterly,* 39(4), 376-379.

41. Diamond, W. & Pease, B. (2001). 'Digital reference: a case study of question types in an academic library.' *Reference Services Review,* 29(3), 210-218.

42. Garnsey, B. & Powell, R.R. *Ibid.*

43. Janes, J., Hill, C., & Rolfe, A. *Ibid.*

44. McClennen, M. & Memmot, P. (2001). 'Roles in digital reference.' *Information Technology and Libraries,* September, 143-148.

45. Garnsey, B. & Powell, R.R. *Ibid.*

46. Janes, J. (2002). 'Digital reference: reference librarians' experiences and attitudes.' *Journal of the American Society for Information Science and Technology,* 53(7), 549-566.

47. Bushallow-Wilber, L., DeVinney, G. & Whitcomb, F. (1996). 'Electronic mail reference service: a study.' *RQ*, 35(3), 359-70.

48. Gray, S. *Ibid.*

49. Jesudason, M. (2000). 'Outreach to student-athletes through e-mail reference service.' *Reference Services Review*, 28(3), 262-267.

50. Powell, C.A. & Bradigan, P.S. (2001). 'E-mail reference services: characteristics and effects at an academic health sciences library.' *Reference & User Services Quarterly*, 41(2), 170-178.

51. Roysdon, C.M. & Elliott, L.L. (1988). 'Electronic integration of library services through a campuswide network.' *RQ*, 28, 82-93.

52. Schilling-Eccles, K. & Harzbecker, J.J. (1998). 'The use of electronic mail at the reference desk: impact of a computer-mediated communication technology on librarian-client interactions.' *Medical Reference Services Quarterly*, 17(4), 17-27.

53. O'Neill, N. (1999). 'E-mail reference service in the public library: a virtual necessity.' *Public Libraries*, September/October.

54. Diamond, W. & Pease, B. (2001). *Ibid.*

55. Dilevko, J. & Gottlieb, L. (2002). 'Print sources in an electronic age: a vital part of the research process for undergraduate students.' *The Journal of Academic Librarianship*, 28(6), 381-392.

56. Tenopir, C. (2001). 'Virtual reference services in a real world.' *Library Journal*, July, 38-39.

57. Wilson, M.C. (2000). 'Evolution or entropy? Changing reference/user culture and the future of reference librarians.' *Reference and User Services Quarterly*, 39 (4), 387-390.

58. Gray, S. (2000). *Ibid.*

59. Janes, J. (2002). *Ibid.*

60. Lipow, A.G. (1999). " 'In your face' reference service.' *Library Journal*, 124 (13), 50-53.

61. Tenopir, C. (2001). *Ibid.*

62. Bowman, V. (2002). 'The virtual librarian and the electronic reference interview.' *Internet Reference Services Quarterly*, 7(3), 3-14.

63. Schwartz, J. (2002). 'Internet access and end-user needs.' *Reference & User Services Quarterly*, 41(3), 253-263, p. 253.

64. D'Elia, G., Jorgensen, C., & Woelfel, J. (2002). 'The impact of the Internet on public library use: an analysis of the current consumer market for library and Internet services.' *Journal of the American Society for Information Science and Technology*, 53(10), 802-820.

65. Desai, C.M. (2003). 'Instant messaging reference: how does it compare?' *The Electronic Library*, 21:1, 21-30.

66. D'Elia, G. et al. (2002). *Ibid.*, pp. 809-810.

67. Bowman, V. (2002). *Ibid.*

68. Jones, S. (2002). *The Internet goes to College: How Students Are Living in the Future with Today's Technology*. Washington: Pew Internet & American Life Project. Available electronically from <http://www.pewinternet.org/reports/pdfs/PIP_College_Report.pdf>. Accessed October 29, 2002.

69. Gray, S. (2000). *Ibid.*

70. Janes, J. & Hill (2001). *Ibid.*

71. Lipow, A.G. (2002). 'Point-of-need reference service: no longer an after-thought.' RUSA Forum: The Future of Reference, 1-7. Available electronically from <http://www.ala.org/rusa/forums/lipow.pdf>. Accessed August 19, 2002.

72. Rettig, J. (2002). 'Technology, cluelessness, anthropology, and the Memex: the future of academic reference service.' RUSA Forum: The Future of Reference, 1-7. Available electronically from <http://www.ala.org/rusa/forums/rettig.pdf>. Accessed August 19, 2002.

73. Tyckoson, D. (2002). 'On the desirableness of personal relations between librarians and readers: the past and future of reference service.' RUSA Forums: The Future of Reference, 1-7. Available electronically from <http://www.ala.org/rusa/forums/tyckoson.pdf>. Accessed August 19, 2002.

74. Missingham, R. (2000). 'Virtual services for virtual readers: reference reborn in the E-library.' Paper presented at Capitalising on Knowledge: The Information Profession in the 21st Century. Annual Conference of the Australian Library and Information Association. October 24-26. Available electronically from <http://www.alia.org.au/conferences/alia2000/proceedings/roxanne.missingham.html>. Accessed May 30, 2002.

75. Goetsch, L., Sowers, L, & Todd, C. (1999). 'SPEC kit 251. Electronic reference service October 1999, executive summary.' Available electronically from <http://www.arl.org/spec/251sum.html>. Accessed August 19, 2002.

76. Stacy-Bates, K.K. (2000). 'Ready-reference resources and e-mail reference on academic ARL Web sites.' *Reference & User Services Quarterly*, 40(1), 61-73.

77. Janes, J. & Silverstein, J. (2003). *Ibid.*

78. Garnsey, B. & Powell, R.R. (2000). *Ibid,* p. 248.

79. O'Neill, N. (1999). *Ibid,* 302-303.

80. O'Neill, N. (2003, February 26.) _Re: [DIG_REF] impact of digital reference services_. Available e-mail: <LISTSERV@LISTSERV.SYR.EDU>. Available electronically from <http://groups.yahoo.com/group/dig_ref/post.html>. Accessed March 3, 2003.

81. Janes, J. & Hill, C. (2002). 'Finger on the pulse: librarians describe evolving reference practice in an increasingly digital world.' *Reference & User Services Quarterly*, 42(1), 54-65.

82. Oder, N. (2003). *Ibid.*

83. Lankes, R.D. & Shostack, P. (2002). 'The necessity of real-time: fact and fiction in digital reference systems.' *Reference & User Services Quarterly*, 41(4), 350-355.

84. Tomer, C. (1994). 'MIME and electronic reference services.' *The Reference Librarian*, 41/42, 347-373, p. 367.

85. Lankes, R.D. (1998). "Building and Maintaining Internet Information Services: K-12 Digital Reference Services." *ERIC Clearinghouse on Information & Technology.* Syracuse, NY.

86. Sloan, B. (2001). 'Ready for reference: academic libraries offer live web-based reference: evaluation system use.' Available electronically from <http://www.lis.uiuc.edu/~b-sloan/ready4ref.htm>. Accessed September 10, 2002.

87. Bushallow-Wilber, L. et al., (1996). *Ibid.*

88. McGlinchey, S. (2002). 'Ask a Librarian report July 2001-December 2001.' Available electronically from <http://www.libraries.vic.gov.au/asklibrarian/AskAlibrep012002.doc>. Accessed September 10, 2002.

89. Lederer, N. (2001). *Ibid*, p. 67.

90. Roysdon, C.M. & Elliott, L.L. (1988). *Ibid*, p. 85.

91. McGlinchey, S. (2002). *Ibid*, p. 1.

92. Fitzgerald, B. & McGlinchey, S. (2001). *Ibid*, p. 11.

93. McGlinchey, S. (2002). *Ibid*, p. 2.

94. *Ibid*, p. 4.

95. Carter, D.S. & Janes, J. (2000). 'Unobtrusive data analysis of digital reference questions and service at the Internet Public Library: an exploratory study.' *Library Trends*, Fall, 251-265.

96. Sibley, K. (2000). 'Libraries test e-mail reference services: Canada to participate in pilot project for global network.' *Quill & Quire*, July.

97. Boyd, C. (2002). 'Ramsey County: Got a question? Ask an e-librarian.' *Saint Paul Pioneer Press (Minnesota),* April 1.

98. Fitzgerald, B. & McGlinchey, S. (2001). *Ibid*, p. 9.

99. Childers, T., Lopata, C. & Stafford, B. (1991). 'Measuring the difficulty of reference questions.' *RQ*, 31(2), 237-244.

100. Rettig, J. (1991). 'Reference research questions.' *RQ*, 31(2), 167-8.

101. Janes, J. (2002). 'Digital reference: reference librarians' experiences and attitudes.' *Journal of the American Society for Information Science and Technology*, 53(7), 549-566.

102. Stover, M. (2000). 'Reference librarians and the Internet: a qualitative study.' *Reference Services Review*, 28(1), 39-46.

103. Jesudason, M. (2000). *Ibid*, p. 267.

104. Cunningham, S.J. (1998). 'Providing Internet reference service for the New Zealand Digital Library: gaining insight into the user base for a digital library.' Available electronically from: <http://web.simmons.edu/~chen/nit/NIT'98/98-027-Cunningham. html>. Accessed August 15, 2002.

105. Botts, C. (1999). 'Reference issues exploration: electronic mail reference service.' Available electronically from <http://www.unm.edu/~rebs/e-mailref/paper.html>. Accessed May 15, 2002.

106. Shalat, H. (2003, February 21.) _Re: [DIG_REF] E-mail reference: alive and kicking.' Available e-mail: <LISTSERV@LISTSERV.SYR.EDU>. Available electronically from <http://groups.yahoo.com/group/dig_ref/post.html>. Accessed March 3, 2003.

107. Hegenbart, B. (1998). 'The economics of the Internet Public Library.' *The Economics of the Internet*, 62:2, 69-83.

108. Bristow, A. (1992). *Ibid.*

109. Ryan, S. (1996). *Ibid.*

110. Hegenbart, B. (1998). *Ibid*, p. 79.

111. McKinzie, S. (2002). 'Virtual Reference: Overrated, Inflated, and Not Even Real.' *The Charleston Advisor*, 4 (2), October.

112. Boese, K.C. (Ed.). (2002). 'If you want my 2¢ worth.' *The Bottom Line: Managing Library Finances*, 15 (2).

113. Garnsey, B. & Powell, R.R. (2000). *Ibid.*

114. Diamond, W. & Pease, B. (2001). *Ibid.*

115. Powell, C.A. & Bradigan, P.S. (2001). *Ibid.*

116. Diamond, W. & Pease, B. (2001). *Ibid*, p. 211.

117. Richardson, J., Fletcher, J., Hunter, A. & Westerman, P. (2000). 'Ask a Librarian' electronic reference services: the importance of corporate culture, communication and service attitude.' *LASIE*, December, 25-37.

118. Katz, B. (2001). 'Long live old reference services and new technologies.' *Library Trends*, 50(2), 263-289, p. 270.

119. Awcock, F.H. (2001). 'Transforming centres of excellence: the State Library of Victoria's challenge.' *Library Review*, 50(7/8), 355-365, p. 364.

120. Jesty, L. (2001). 'Receiving, responding to and recording research and reference questions enquiries electronically-the new 3Rs in enquiry services.' Available electronically from <http://www.vala.org.au/vala2002/2002pdf/19Jesty.pdf>. Accessed 26 January, 2002.

SECTION TWO:
HOW WE DO IT HERE

Predicting the Success
of Commercial AskA Services
in the United States and Abroad

Jenny Baum
Kate Lyons

SUMMARY. This article discusses the quality of commercial and library-sponsored AskA services and uses this as a prediction for the
success of the programs. The authors also explore the idea of the

Jenny Baum (E-mail: jenny.baum@earthlink.net or jennybaum@nypl.org) is Librarian and Kate Lyons (E-mail: kate.lyons@earthlink.net or clyons@nypl.org) is
Information Literacy Specialist II, both with the New York Public Library's Click on @ the
library digital divide initiative.
    Address correspondence to: Jenny Baum and/or Kate Lyons, 579 West 215th Street
#6G, New York, NY 10034.

    [Haworth co-indexing entry note]: "Predicting the Success of Commercial AskA Services in the United
States and Abroad." Baum, Jenny, and Kate Lyons. Co-published simultaneously in *The Reference Librarian*
(The Haworth Information Press, an imprint of The Haworth Press, Inc.) No. 85, 2004, pp. 81-89; and: *Digital
versus Non-Digital Reference: Ask a Librarian Online and Offline* (ed: Jessamyn West) The Haworth Information Press, an imprint of The Haworth Press, Inc., 2004, pp. 81-89. Single or multiple copies of this article
are available for a fee from The Haworth Document Delivery Service [1-800-HAWORTH, 9:00 a.m. - 5:00
p.m. (EST). E-mail address: docdelivery@haworthpress.com].

Digital Object Identifer: 10.1300/J120v41n85_06   *81* commoditization of information and its acceptance rates in different countries, and use these to predict the success of commercial and library-sponsored AskA services both in the United States and abroad. *[Article copies available for a fee from The Haworth Document Delivery Service: 1-800-HAWORTH. E-mail address: <docdelivery@haworthpress.com> Website: <http://www.HaworthPress.com> © 2004 by The Haworth Press, Inc. All rights reserved.]*

KEYWORDS. AskA, online reference, international AskA programs, information brokerage

You have a question. You need an answer. Maybe you don't have time to do the search yourself. Or, maybe you're unsure of the best way to go about your search. You decide that you need an information professional, and that you want to interface with this person via online communications, like a web-board, chat or e-mail. You could go to one of the many library sponsored online reference services to Ask a Librarian for free, or you could go to a for-profit site and pay for help.

Searching through Google Answers, a fee-based, virtual reference service, it's clear that some people choose to pay for commercial AskA services. Commercial question boards are full of users asking questions and commenting on other users' questions. The services are not deserted and unused. Perhaps these commercial reference services will become wildly popular, while library online reference services sit idle. Today we take the part of fortune teller and try to predict the success of the commercial and library-sponsored programs, based on the quality of their services and the popular perceptions about the commodization of information.

Ann Marie Parsons ends her article, "Digital Reference: How Libraries Can Compete with AskA Services" (2001) with the following statement:

> If librarians create standards for how and when quality information will be delivered to patrons educated with the knowledge of what information to accept and from whom, libraries will no longer be beholden to the standards set by AskA services. Instead AskA services will find it necessary to keep up with libraries.

Now, two years after Ann Marie Parson's article, librarians can reflect on how their own digital reference services have evolved, and compare their work to that of commercial services. Generally, library sponsored online reference sources meet all the criteria for satisfying a user's information needs.

Library AskA services are often better established than for-profit AskA services, partly due to the fact that they have more combined global resources. According to Kasowitz, in 1999, "45% of academic libraries (Janes, Carter, and Memmott, 1999) and 13% of public libraries (Janes, 2001) offered digital reference services through e-mail and the Web" and that "a later study found that 99% of 70 academic libraries offer e-mail reference and 29% offer real-time reference service" (Tenopir, 2001).

In the U.S., the Collaborative Digital Reference Service (CDRS), <http://www.loc.gov/loc/lcib/01078/reference.html>, seeks to link academic, public and governmental libraries and the Virtual Reference Desk (VRD) "consists of almost twenty AskA services (specializing in science, math, education, art, general reference, and other areas) that submit out-of-scope and overflow questions via e-mail to VRD to be redistributed to other member services or answered by librarian volunteers" (Kasowitz, 2001). Librarians are filling the need for these services. CDRS launched a collaborative site by librarians for librarians, called QuestionPoint.org. Their "Global Network" lets the user choose the question language and reply language.

These services in particular, and libraries in general, have channeled their organization's efforts towards smoothing the mechanics of AskA service, meeting the criteria for finding an information professional, and bridging cultural and language barriers. The type of service that library-sponsored online reference services are able to provide, a global network of other information professionals, about their online reference projects and each other's, gives library-sponsored online reference services an added edge, a collaboration between peers that competitive commercial businesses often lack.

Libraries have made steps towards smoothing the mechanics of information service. The tradition of reference librarianship has paved the way for new technology standards among AskA services. However, technology standards have yet to be established between AskA services, much less international AskA services. Kasowitz defines this problem as including "specifications for expressing, sharing and storing data captured in digital reference transactions (i.e., question-answer exchanges)."

There are several criteria for finding an information professional. Commercial services have been participating in information brokerage for years, for the medical and law professions. Only recently have commercial services sought to answer the information needs of Everyman. While the information needs of the average user may not appear to be as crucial as in a medical or law setting, the accuracy of the information is always of the utmost importance to the person receiving it, especially since users may use online information to make critical life decisions. Imagine a user on an online question board asking for advice on whether to visit a doctor, given a set of symptoms, or whether they need counseling for a problem. A typical consumer needs accurate, objective information as much as any business or corporate user. Cultural and language barriers are an obstacle to providing patrons with their information, that information professionals face regardless of whether they answer reference questions over the phone, online or in-person.

Cultural and language barriers cannot be addressed as thoroughly online as they can be in a library setting. The Web is notoriously English-based and America-centric. The United States accounts for 29% of global Internet access according to the Nielson/Netratings report for 2/20/03 (*Library Journal*, April, 2003). This is a large percentage for one country, but is still only a fraction of who's online. While Google and Babblefish translators have helped to bridge language barriers, there is simply not the wealth of information available online in other languages that is available in book resources and proprietary databases in English. If the user is not a native English speaker, or if there is some cultural dynamic to their question, the user may also lose out on making their questions fully understood. The potential for an erroneous or misleading answer is that much higher in an online setting. Reference question leads such as body language and inflection cannot be conveyed as accurately online as they can in a face-to-face interview. Because librarians have so much experience with in-person reference interviews, they may be more sensitive to realizing these differences between electronic reference and in-person references, and are great candidates for figuring out how to adapt to the electronic reference interview. One criteria for comparing information professionals might be this experience with a diverse patronage, both in face-to-face reference interviews and in cyberspace.

Commercial AskA services in the United States have tried to smooth the mechanics of AskA service, meet the criteria for finding an information professional, and bridge cultural and language barriers by emulating the library's question board services. In doing so, commercial enterprises changed certain aspects of the online reference interview. For example, online for-profit services often only check online resources, can pick and choose the questions they want to answer, have employees that may or may not be certified librarians, do not offer phone support, and refer patrons to the sources that provide the best domain names regardless of whether they are the best resources. Unlike libraries, commercial services can often provide marketing for their services that libraries cannot. Unfortunately, overzealous marketing can sometimes extend to commercial AskA results. Moreover, for-profit search engines, such as Google and Ask Jeeves, have been known to change search results that do not reflect well on the company, or that are perceived as not being conducive to a search (Tomaiulo). Most users would agree that having a company with outside agendas censor their results does not make for the best information professional.

Lisa Guernsey's *New York Times* article in 2000, "Suddenly, Everybody's an Expert on Everything," states "An expert, it seems, is now an ordinary person sitting at home, beaming advice over the Internet to anyone who wants help" (http://www.william.russo.com/timesarticle. htm). In examining criteria for choosing an Information Professional, we can better understand other qualities required in an online reference librarian. Besides the ability to work with a diverse patronage, the Information Professional must have access to the most diverse and most authoritative information, be familiar with all of the available resources, be readily available (return answers quickly), motivated to answer all questions equally, and thoroughly understand the question (be a good reference interviewer).

The question of whether a researcher on a commercial AskA site has access to more information than a typical AskA librarian depends both on the library-sponsored AskA program and on the researcher working for a commercial AskA service. Typically, a librarian would have access to all of their information available at their library, including the Internet, and all other library materials and electronic resources. A Google Researcher, for example, might also have access to all the library resources their local, academic, or corporate library provides, but it is also possible that they only have access to the World Wide Web for their information. Thus, a user choosing between a commercial or a library-sponsored AskA service who is concerned that their researcher definitely has access to the largest collection, might be more likely to choose a library AskA service than a commercial AskA service.

Users may realize, however, that regardless of the quantity of information an information professional has at their fingertips, their ability to search through their information vastly impacts the quality of their answer. The FAQ on Google Answers states the following, in response to a question about the expertise of their Researchers:

> All Google Researchers are tested to ensure that they are expert searchers with excellent communication skills. Some of them also have expertise in various fields. Your question may be answered by an expert in a particular field or by an expert searcher. (http://answers.google.com/answers/faq.html)

The Google FAQ continues with an explanation about an essay researchers must write, and practical experience they need, with answering sample questions. Also, Google provides their users with a "money-back guarantee." The screening process for a librarian position is not only more rigorous, but also more standard. Most library reference positions require their staff to have Master's Degrees from accredited universities. Accreditation establishes a standard. A user concerned that the person answering their question is the most skilled at finding information, might be more likely to choose a library service, where the user is assured that every librarian meets these standards. A user choosing a commercial AskA service may or may not find similar standards.

Users may also worry that the person answering their question determines how much time to spend on the question, and how thoroughly to answer, based on the complexity of the question. The professional answering the question, who is paid hourly or on salary, will not have any financial motivation for answering one question more thoroughly than any other. Users who cannot afford to offer as much money for an answer to their question, will find that library-based AskA services will be more in their price ranges.

A user concerned that the person answering their question takes the time to conduct a reference interview and thoroughly understand a question before answering might find that a library service would better suit their needs. Again, a researcher paid on a per-question basis might invest less time and energy into a question, because they know that the outcome would be less.

Despite their drawbacks, it appears that people will pay for what AskA services offer. As mentioned earlier, the commercial sites are not languishing unused. North Americans accept the idea of information as a commodity, and we're willing to pay for services that were once free. However, if services like Google Answers do not provide better service than libraries, it is unlikely that they will succeed globally, unless people perceive that they get more by paying.

From medicine and food to education and recreation, everything in American society is a commodity. Just as every aspect of American life has been commoditized, so has our access to information. In its mission statement, The New York Public Library states that it "provides free and open access to the accumulated wisdom of the world, without distinction as to income, religion, nationality, or other human condition." Public libraries are built on the principle of free and equal access to information. However, people in the United States are more accustomed to paying for services.

. International libraries, despite different adoption rates of Internet technologies, often seem to lean towards the free and democratic distribution of information, even as for-profit services gain footholds in their countries.

In Norway, the service "Harde Fakta" (Hard Facts) was established to sell information on regional trade and industry. Their public library rules and regulations required that the service be changed to a free system (Lamvik, 1996). Another Norwegian for-profit based system is the INFOSOK project. This project focuses on engineering special libraries and the team leaders carry degrees in multiple fields in order to be more authoritative. According to the International Federation of Library Associations and Institutions (IFLA), Norway's Act on Library Services, amended in 1997, aims to make "all suitable material available free of charge to all those who live in Norway." Norway public libraries have moved away from a fee-based system in favor of an open-access system <http://www.ifla.org/V/cdoc/norway.htm>.

In Sweden, democratic principles also encourage the nonprofit services, like the library's, to thrive. BTJ (Bibliotekstjanst, or Library Service) is a company dealing with services to libraries, they have recently started or will soon start a for-profit AskA service. Some Swedish libraries have an "ask a librarian service" on their web sites, but the perceived trend is that users prefer talking to a librarian by phone or visiting the library, even if the service is free. Birgitta Sandell of Uppsala University Library wrote, in an e-mail to the authors, that "the Swedish policy is that libraries should keep traditional free services. However, companies have to pay for special services and at the Stockholm University Library students have to pay for lending course e-books [. . .] Inter-lending loans outside the Nordic countries also have a charge."

Jesus Lau, of the Special Libraries Association, wrote in an e-mail to the authors that, in Mexico, the consensus is that government, library, education, etc., should all be free, and that this is mainly because of the political climate of the country, the government and policies that they've had for more than 100 years.

In France, the phone-company's Minitel service predates the advent of the Internet. Since Minitel already cost money to use because of the phone company's monopoly, their users are used to the pay system. The convergence of older and newer technologies also means that not everything is on the Internet, as many people are prone to believe. Moreover, many of their libraries do not grant universal access without written permission or do not allow the checking out of books; all books must be read on premises.

In 2000, Gisela Delgado, head of one of Cuba's independent libraries, said of the government, they "consider [independent libraries] to be dissidents, opponents, when all we have wanted to do is promote culture" (source: http://www.cnn.com/2000/WORLD/americas/11/12/reading. freedom.ap/). While the government does not ban books, they are able to control the flow of information by making politically sensitive books harder to find. Allowing various sources of information can make it more difficult to stem the flow of information.

There's nothing new about businesses offering services similar to ones that libraries have traditionally offered for free. And often, there is some added value to fee-based services. For example, video rental stores may have different hours than a user's local library, and the user may decide that convenience is worth a fee. That's the Capitalist view of information services, that weighs perceived value against supply and demand. As a result, the commoditization of information does not strike North Americans as unusual.

In a country that does not offer global health care, global access to information is a desirable, but lofty goal. Charging for access to information is not seen as a sacrifice of democratic principles as long as there is value added by the service. International libraries appear to be more resistant to adopting for-profit services.

Thus, the authors of this paper make their prediction. In the future, and possibly already, library-sponsored online reference and AskA services provide a more desirable service. However, because users are willing to pay for information, and may perceive an added value to the service simply because there is a charge associated with the service, commercial services may succeed in the United States. Within groups of people who are resistant to the commoditization of information, commercial AskA services will not succeed, simply on principle. And, the authors predict that globally, enough areas exist with people resistant to the idea of the commoditization of information, that commercial AskA services will be more successful in the United States than abroad.

BIBLIOGRAPHY

http://www.diglib.org/pubs/news02_01/RefBenchmark.htm.

http://www.william.russo.com/timesarticle.htm.

Kasowitz, Abby S. "Trends and Issues in Digital Reference Services." *ERIC Digest*, November 2001. <http://www.ericit.org/digests/EDO-IR-2001-07.shtml>.

Janes, J. (2001). Current research in digital reference. In A. S. Kasowitz and J. Stahl (Eds.), *Facets of Digital Reference*. [Online]. Available: http://vrd.org/conferences/ VRD2000/proceedings/janes-intro.shtml [September 25, 2001] (IR058319).

Janes, J., Carter, D. S., and Memmott, P. (1999). Digital reference services in academic libraries. *Reference & User Services Quarterly*, 39 (2), 145-150.

Lamvik, Aud. "Information Brokerage Activities in Norway." *Information Services & Use*, 1996, Vol 16 Issue 2, p. 145.

Library Journal. April 15, 2003. Volume 128, No. 7.

Mayfield, Kendra. "Ask a Librarian, Not Jeeves." *Wired News* <http://www.wired. com/news/culture/0,1284,40308,00.html>.

Tenopir, C. (2001). Virtual reference services in a real world. *Library Journal*, 126 (11) 38-40.

Tomaiulo, Nicolas G. (2000). "Aska and You May Receive: Commercial Reference Services on the Web." *Searcher*, May 2000, Vol. 8 Issue 5, p. 56.

West, Jessamyn (2002). "Information for Sale: My Experience with Google Answers" *Searcher*, Oct. 2002, Vol. 10 Issue 9, p. 14.

Wired New Jersey:
Q and A NJ

Carol Van Houten

SUMMARY. Q and A NJ is New Jersey's virtual reference service. Available 24 hours a day, seven days a week, and free to all New Jersey residents, the service provides online reference assistance in real time from librarians across the state. New Jersey was the first state in the country to offer such service. This article looks at the history of the service, what it's like to be a virtual librarian, and presents a brief survey of the librarians participating in Q and A NJ. *[Article copies available for a fee from The Haworth Document Delivery Service: 1-800-HAWORTH. E-mail address: <docdelivery@haworthpress.com> Website: <http://www.HaworthPress. com> © 2004 by The Haworth Press, Inc. All rights reserved.]*

KEYWORDS. Virtual reference, electronic information resource searching, information services, libraries, computer software

"Ding dong." Sounding much like the doors of a subway closing, the two-toned chime signals the arrival of a new patron with a question for a

Carol Van Houten is a reference librarian and publishes the website, *The Constant Reader* <http://www.constantreader.org>.

Address correspondence to: Carol Van Houten, 213 Seventh Street #3, Jersey City, NJ 07302 (E-mail: carol@constantreader.org).

[Haworth co-indexing entry note]: "Wired New Jersey: Q and A NJ." Van Houten, Carol. Co-published simultaneously in *The Reference Librarian* (The Haworth Information Press, an imprint of The Haworth Press, Inc.) No. 85, 2004, pp. 91-100; and: *Digital versus Non-Digital Reference: Ask a Librarian Online and Offline* (ed: Jessamyn West) The Haworth Information Press, an imprint of The Haworth Press, Inc., 2004, pp. 91-100. Single or multiple copies of this article are available for a fee from The Haworth Document Delivery Service [1-800-HAWORTH, 9:00 a.m. - 5:00 p.m. (EST). E-mail address: docdelivery@haworthpress. com].

librarian. The patron could be in Cape May, or Edison, or Jersey City. And the librarian who answers may be in Newark, or Jackson, or Vineland. But they won't be in the same place, at the same time.

Can you find me a timeline of the life of Helen Keller?

This and thousands of other questions have been ably and professionally answered by librarians across the state of New Jersey participating in the statewide online reference service, Q and A NJ. Free and available 24/7 to all New Jersey residents, the service is staffed by librarians in 34 (and counting) library systems statewide. Having answered more than 5,900 questions during the month of March, 2003, Q and A NJ can rightly claim to be the busiest online reference service in the world.

HISTORY OF THE SERVICE

Q and A NJ began as the result of a brainstorming session in South Jersey. The South Jersey Regional Library Cooperative (SJRLC), which serves libraries in seven southern counties, was looking for a way to reach more patrons and promote library services in a new and innovative way. Peter Bromberg, Program Coordinator for SJRLC, explained that the organizers saw it as a way to renew the leadership role for reference librarians, and "showcase the expertise of library staff."

Out of initial meetings in January, 2000, the idea grew into finding things that would "surprise and delight users" and building a marketing campaign around "one amazing thing that libraries do," according to Bromberg. That one thing became answering reference questions. The amazing part turned out to be doing it online, in a "chat" format. By September, the group had settled on reference services through the Web and began creating a pilot project with ten South Jersey libraries participating. The coordinators chose Library Systems and Services Inc.'s (LSSI) Virtual Reference Desk software as the project's software platform because, Bromberg explains, "it had performed well in a demonstration, and was also the only viable product on the market" at the time.

The project applied for and received Library Services and Technology Act (LSTA) federal funding, and went live to the public on October 1, 2001, making it the first statewide online reference service in the country. Staffing is provided by the ever-growing number of participating libraries; presently, 34 library systems and more than 250 librarians participate. After four months of weekday service, the program expanded to 24/7 coverage. Overnight and Sunday hours are presently covered by LSSI librarians. That, however, may change. According to Bromberg, "LSSI's Web Reference Center has generally done a good job, but the long-term goal is to staff more hours with NJ librarians. In addition to better coordinating quality control, having more shifts staffed by NJ librarians would fulfill another project goal: providing staff development opportunities."

Organizationally speaking, the project uses face-to-face meetings as well as a good deal of technology to keep things running smoothly. Each participating library has a Q and A project manager. The group uses an online calendar to coordinate coverage and swap shifts, if necessary. Most of the libraries I contacted contribute six hours of coverage per week, in three two-hour shifts. There also are two listservs that participants use to communicate new issues and concerns. Additionally, the training manual and lots of ready reference suggestions are all available online to the participating librarians.

The growth of the service has been astounding. During the first full month of service, October 2001, Q and A answered 451 questions. By October 2002 that number had increased to 3,774–a 600% increase in usage. Marketing for the service has included links on the home page of participating libraries, bookmarks distributed at schools and bookstores, and probably most important, word of mouth. Public response has been overwhelmingly positive. Satisfaction is tracked through patron feedback forms, which initially yielded a 35% response rate. To date, 91% of patrons say they would use the service again and 80% said they were satisfied with the service.

Q AND A IN ACTION

I spent a morning with Dale Colston and Leslie Kahn, two librarians at Newark Public Library who support the service on Saturday mornings. The first thing I noticed was that they both were having a good time. Librarians by their nature get a kick out of answering questions–but working online adds an extra element of challenge and fun to the process. Colston easily juggled multiple open windows on her desktop: several browser windows for performing searches, the Virtual Reference Desk (VRD) software window showing messages scrolling down from a patron, and another window showing the queue of other patrons waiting for help. Colston, who's been answering questions for the service for a year, agreed that it is as fun as it looks.

The VRD software allows the librarian to "push" a web page to the patron's screen. The program uses a split screen format, so patrons can see the page of information from the librarian, while at the same time along the right hand side of the screen there is an area devoted to the scrolling chat between librarian and patron.

While most people are very appreciative of the service, Colston mentioned that people feel freer to be rude online than they ever would be in person. Additionally, the anonymity introduces more personal questions, about things like taxes, legal issues, or sexuality. If a patron asks a purely salacious question, like, "what are you wearing," librarians can end the session with a scripted message that's part of the software which says "You are using inappropriate language . . . I'm logging off now."

And then there are the students. Colston remembered the time she realized an entire class had logged on together, "when I was suddenly asked 'what was the cause of the fall of the Roman Empire' a dozen times." During the busiest time periods, there may be four or five librarians staffing the service. But just like at the brick and mortar library, class visits need to be scheduled in advance. Recently the service added Tutor.com for live free homework help for students. This is a separate outside service which is not staffed by librarians. Kahn explained that librarians act as intermediaries, though, since sometimes a student may think they need a tutor when they actually just have a quick reference question. Students who request live homework help are first directed to Q and A NJ librarians; then if the librarian deems it is a tutoring related request rather than an information request, the student is redirected to Tutor.com.

During my hour with Kahn, her questions included:

> How would I find a list of business associations in New Jersey?
> Does the phrase 'puritanical society' have to be capitalized?
> Does the Internet keep track of people's birthdays?
> I have to learn how to draw a dragon . . .

I expected to see lots of reference books piled around the terminal where she answers questions, but she only had a few: a good dictionary, an almanac, the *Encyclopedia of Associations*; plus, plenty of printed finding aids to web sites that have been useful in the past, particularly for children's sites. There are a great number of school-aged children using the service. Both Kahn and Colston agreed that 90 to 95 percent of the questions posed can be answered using online resources. The nature of the service is to answer quick, ready-reference type questions. In-depth research questions usually get a few starting points, and suggestions about places to continue the research (a particular library collection, perhaps). If a librarian knows a question is too in-depth to answer in real time, they can offer to e-mail a response to a patron in a stated amount of time. Kahn answered all of her questions but one during the session. For that one, she wanted to use print sources, so she offered to e-mail a response by the end of the day, and the patron was satisfied with that. Kahn mentioned that the real time format does make it difficult to use print sources, which is troubling since they are sometimes the best way to answer a question.

Online reference in real time serves as a bridge to reaching web-surfing-obsessed patrons. As Kahn said, "With the Internet, so many people aren't asking librarians questions anymore–so the (Q and A NJ) service is wonderful because it shows that people still want to ask librarians questions. And we can show them how great librarians really are."

Generally speaking, it is the younger patrons, who grew up with instant messaging, chat rooms, and immediate gratification, who expect responses to be magically instantaneous. They can be trying to deal with, particularly when they send messages like, "Hurry up! You're so slooooooow! What's taking you so long?" As a former children's librarian, I can vouch for the fact that even the most aggressive kid in the library would never speak to a librarian this way in person. On the other hand, Kahn's young patron who needed step-by-step instructions for drawing a dragon was effusive with praise when the web site she needed appeared on her terminal, thanks to Kahn's diligent search. "Leslie, you're the greatest! Thank you soooooo much!!" On this particular Saturday morning, the satisfied patrons far outweighed the grumblers. And as Kahn noted, some people are never satisfied. Just like in real life.

Q AND A: THE SURVEY

I conducted a brief, informal survey via e-mail of the Q and A NJ participating libraries to see what they thought about working the virtual reference desk. Out of 33 libraries, I received 13 responses, including one from the LSSI Web Reference Center staff. One librarian at Princeton Public Library made an interesting point:

"Virtual reference" is a misnomer. There's nothing virtual about it. The people who use it have real questions and the Q and A NJ librarians use real research and communications skills to provide real answers. We're just taking advantage of technology to extend and expand the reference service we have traditionally provided.

The libraries that responded to my survey were:

Burlington County College
Camden County Library System
Gloucester County College
LSSI Web Reference Center
Millburn Free Public Library
New Brunswick Public Library
New Jersey State Library
Newark Public Library
Piscataway Public Library
Princeton Public Library
University of Medicine and Dentistry of New Jersey
Vineland Public Library
Woodbridge Public Library

Here are the questions I asked and a summary of the answers.

Question One: How many questions does your library answer for Q and A NJ on a typical day?

The responses to this question varied from 4 to 28. The average of the answers was 9.7 questions answered. The real answer is, it depends on the shift. Early evening, when young people are working on homework, is far busier than, say, the middle of the day.

Question Two: How does answering a question online differ from answering a reference question in person? What are the special challenges?

Answers are in order of frequency that they were mentioned.

1. Missing body language, non-verbal cues, the challenge of not being face to face (8 responses)
2. Reference interview is more difficult online, people are less able to express themselves clearly through writing/typing challenges (7 responses)

3. Anonymity of patron leads to abuse of librarian: rudeness, inappropriate questions (6 responses)
4. "Dead air" problem: keeping people engaged/aware that you are still searching for them by using chat function (5 responses)
5. Demand for "instant gratification" more apparent (5 responses)
6. The technology itself is challenging: the software, slow Internet connections, disconnects (3 responses)
7. Makes using print sources harder (2 responses)
8. Makes dealing with multiple patrons more difficult than in person (1 response)

Question 3: Do people ask different types of questions online as compared to in person? Any examples?

Answers are in order of frequency that they were mentioned.

1. Questions are the same as in person, covering a wide variety of topics (6 responses)
2. There are more inappropriate questions (i.e., "what are you wearing") (5 responses)
3. Questions are more random than I am accustomed to in my library, due to the broader range of patrons asking them; different customer base (the entire state rather than one town) (2 responses)
4. People are more likely to ask multiple questions online than in person (2 responses)
5. Questions are haphazard; not well thought out (1 response)
6. Questions are more likely to be answerable via online sources (1 response)

Examples of the types of questions asked (which illustrates similarity to questions asked in person): song lyrics, biographies, directions, homework help, book/movie reviews, health, sexuality, emotional support/cries for help, recipes, taxes, genealogy, history.

Question 4: Do you think the diverse population in New Jersey is well-served by Q and A NJ? For instance, what provisions are available for patrons who pose questions in languages other than English?

Answers to this question varied widely. Here are some samples.

If the librarian who takes the call is not able to answer the question, it will be forwarded to someone who can.

We are getting questions from people of all ages and walks of life.

Some of the librarians who do Q and A NJ are able to communicate in other languages including Spanish.

Someone at my library has twice answered in Spanish.

We also lack assistance to low-vision/blind people, I think.

This is an evolving service; if it expands, I expect it will include more resources geared to non-English speakers . . . the project really is still in its early stages.

As far as economic diversity, the fact that the service can be accessed from library workstations helps serve the population that may not have computers in the home.

Q and A is highly praised by the elderly and disabled because information services are brought to the patron.

The language problem is one that concerns me. . . . I understand some French and Spanish, but not enough to quickly interpret a question. There are growing Chinese and Russian populations here in my town as well as the Indian and Pakistani communities. At this moment, they are served primarily by having someone else who understands English assist them.

The senior population also concerns me, since I think there is still a problem with getting many older patrons to use computers, period.

On this question, Bromberg said, "We are just now beginning to explore offering a Spanish language service. This may be something we see in late 2003 or 2004. We have to look at demand and funding issues."

Question 5: What has the response been from users of the service?

The answer to this question was essentially unanimous: overwhelmingly positive and appreciative. Comments included:

They are impressed by the speed, accuracy, availability and professionalism of the service.

People are amazed and very thankful.

For some customers, this is the first time that they realize that librarians will help answer questions.

The convenience of contacting a librarian for assistance at any hour from their home is paramount.

Customers are thrilled with the opportunity to interact with a librarian 24 hours a day, seven days a week.

There was general agreement on many things about the service, but at the same time, some statements directly conflicted with one another. For instance, some librarians reported senior citizens said they loved using the service, while other librarians felt the service excluded seniors because of the technology. The anonymity of asking a question online encouraged some patrons to be rude or thoughtless. At the same time, the anonymity also gave shy patrons a platform from which to ask questions, something they might never have done in person. Some librarians felt that patrons who used the service didn't want to "chit-chat," the way they might in person; while others got the impression that if they didn't "chit-chat" the patron would think they were no longer there, at the other end, working on the question.

Several librarians mentioned that young people don't really seem to understand that it is a person at the other end helping them, and not just the computer. This would explain their desire for "instant" results, and their willingness to use a lot less polite language than they might at the actual library. Adults using the service, who grew up using research tools like print periodical indexes instead of electronic databases, naturally are more accustomed to understanding that research takes time. It isn't magic. Even if it starts to look like magic, with librarians delivering the requested information right onto the computer screen in front of them in a matter of minutes. It's easy to see how a child might divorce this delivery system from involving a human.

Overall, responses from the librarians involved with the project were extremely positive. Almost everyone who responded said they were happy to be involved with it; thought it was helping promote libraries in the state in a positive way; and getting services to people who might not otherwise have been reached. One librarian mentioned that she thought it was an excellent exercise in reference work for her staff. Others were happy to learn the new skill of using the software program. One librarian said that recent bad experiences had made her library question the value of participating. The problems involved many instances of abusive language from patrons on the service. However, even this librarian said that overall the response from users has been positive.

THE FUTURE OF Q AND A NJ

While researching this article, I learned of two more libraries joining the service: William Patterson University and New Jersey City University. As more libraries sign on, word of mouth continues to grow, and usage continues to increase. At this point, it would appear that the sky's the limit. Except, of course, for funding. Bromberg said that they look fine for now. The project currently is funded through 2004, at which point they will need to apply for grants again. Bromberg mentioned that expansions in service, such as service in other languages, will depend on funding and the demand. For now, though, New Jersey can bask in its wired status as the first state to offer virtual reference service to all of its residents, free of charge, 24/7. That's service with a virtual smile from the Garden State! :)

BIBLIOGRAPHY

Bromberg, Peter, Program Development Coordinator for the South Jersey Regional Library Cooperative. E-mail interview. March and April 2003.

Colston, Dale, and Leslie Kahn, Librarians, Newark Public Library. Personal interview. 22 March 2003.

Q and A NJ. Administered by the South Jersey Regional Library Cooperative and the New Jersey Library Network. March 2003 <http://www.qandanj.org>.

Sweet, Marianne, Q and A NJ Project Coordinator. E-mail interview. April 2003.

Library LAWLINE:
Collaborative Virtual Reference
in a Special Library Consortium

Scott Matheson

SUMMARY. This article details the planning, design, and implementation of a collaborative virtual reference project undertaken by a group of law libraries. Service design, scheduling, and software selection are addressed. Outcomes and changes to the service after its first year are outlined, and recommendations are made to those considering implementing similar services. *[Article copies available for a fee from The Haworth Document Delivery Service: 1-800-HAWORTH. E-mail address: <docdelivery@ haworthpress.com> Website: <http://www.HaworthPress.com> © 2004 by The Haworth Press, Inc. All rights reserved.]*

KEYWORDS. Virtual reference, online services, reference instruction, computer mediated instruction, communication systems

In the fall of 2001, reference librarians from the New England Law Library Consortium (NELLCO) began to plan an online reference ser-

Scott Matheson is Visiting Reference Librarian, Lillian Goldman Law Library, Yale Law School.

Address correspondence to: Scott Matheson, 99 Gorham Avenue, Hamden, CT 06514 (E-mail: s.matheson@yale.edu).

[Haworth co-indexing entry note]: "Library LAWLINE: Collaborative Virtual Reference in a Special Library Consortium." Matheson, Scott. Co-published simultaneously in *The Reference Librarian* (The Haworth Information Press, an imprint of The Haworth Press, Inc.) No. 85, 2004, pp. 101-114; and: *Digital versus Non-Digital Reference: Ask a Librarian Online and Offline* (ed: Jessamyn West) The Haworth Information Press, an imprint of The Haworth Press, Inc., 2004, pp. 101-114. Single or multiple copies of this article are available for a fee from The Haworth Document Delivery Service [1-800-HAWORTH, 9:00 a.m. - 5:00 p.m. (EST). E-mail address: docdelivery@haworthpress.com].

http://www.haworthpress.com/web/REF
© 2004 by The Haworth Press, Inc. All rights reserved.
Digital Object Identifer: 10.1300/J120v41n85_08

vice. By the fall of 2002, the first patrons were logging in to get real-time help from a librarian. Unlike services that are provided by a single library or library system, the NELLCO service, called Library LAWLINE, is a joint project of 19 libraries from seven states. The collaborative nature of the project presented special challenges and unique opportunities to participating libraries. A task force of ten librarians and the NELLCO executive director worked over the course of almost a year to design and implement a virtual reference service that overcame the challenges and took advantage of the opportunities of a collaborative service.

SERVICE DESIGN

The service was designed from the beginning to be collaborative. This helped guide some decisions on things like shared service policies, training requirements and scheduling concerns. Even the group's choice of software was influenced by the need for many libraries to work together.

The element of the service that presented the biggest challenge was the collaboration between public and academic law libraries–libraries that have different, sometimes very different, patron bases and service models. The task force considered the differences among the patrons and the issues these differences would raise. In the end, the group decided to take all patrons as one group and have all types of librarians assist all types of patrons.

A two-track service model, where academic patrons would be routed to one librarian and public patrons would be routed to another was considered. The task force decided that leaving the four non-academic libraries to staff one track by themselves would not be feasible. The hours that the non-academic libraries could contribute by themselves would have resulted in a service to the public that was only open a few hours a day. Conversely, some academic participants worried that there would not be enough questions from academic patrons alone to learn anything useful from the year-long pilot.

Although the group decided on only having one big queue of questions from all types of patrons, we wanted to be able to have more than one librarian available to answer questions during the busier times. This meant that we had to determine when we thought there would be sufficient traffic on the service to justify having two librarians waiting to help and when we thought that one could handle all the traffic alone.

Since two librarians were needed for part of the schedule, the service would be available for fewer than total number of staff hours available.

SCHEDULING

The task force began to think about how many hours we could provide the service before we even had a firm number of participating libraries. The first guesses were around twenty hours per week. When we found out that there would be 18 participating libraries, we found we had almost twice as many hours of staff time to work with. Weekday hours were extended and weekends and evening hours were added to get a better picture of when patrons need the service. Many on the task force wanted the service to be open quite late into the evening, but when we compared the hours we wanted to offer service with the hours librarians were willing to work, some adjustment was necessary. Most notably, evening hours were cut back. When it debuted, the service was open 56 hours per week, until 7 p.m. on weekdays and open four hours on both Saturday and Sunday.

Once the service schedule was set, actually scheduling the individual shifts turned out to be a significant task. We posted a web calendar on the project site, and one task force member was charged with scheduling individual shifts. We assigned the shifts as two-hour blocks of time, but these were assigned to a library. Individual libraries often split the two-hour shift between two librarians so that each only had to be tied to a computer for one hour.

Many of the participating libraries are not open after 5 p.m. or on weekends. So weekend hours, the most difficult to fill, fell to a few libraries that had reference staff working weekends and a few librarians who volunteered to provide service on some weekends. Similarly, the 5-7 p.m. shift was usually filled by a library that regularly provided reference service during that time. Later in the pilot, some librarians were able to adjust their schedules to work the evening shifts outside of their regular work hours.

The task force began the project by discouraging "double staffing" that is, having one librarian staff the in-person desk in a library and the virtual desk online at the same time. As the pilot progressed and librarians became more facile with the software, libraries with less in-person traffic began to double staff with relatively few problems. Libraries where in-person traffic was higher continued to have a separate librarian staffing the virtual desk.

SOFTWARE SELECTION

The group examined several different software packages early in the process and settled on licensing the 24/7 virtual reference package. We had no definite ideas about what features we would require and those that would be "deal-breakers" when we began researching software packages. As we worked our way through AIM, LiveAssistance, Rakim, Convey, and other options, we began to develop a list of desired features and those we thought would make the service less attractive to patrons.

We liked packages that allowed us to push pages to a patron's screen, and most everything we looked at did this in some form or another. We liked the ability to co-browse, to actively share web pages between librarian and patron, but were not sure how well it would work for patrons with slower Internet connections. Voice-over-IP was a "gee whiz" feature, but had technical requirements for patron's computers that made it less attractive. Because NELLCO has no technical staff, packages that required local servers and technical expertise were not an option we could pursue. We preferred packages that were hosted on the software vendor's computers. We did not like packages that required patrons to download or install a special program. We thought that this would be a turn-off for many of our patrons, especially public law library patrons who tend to be one-time or occasional library users, not repeat customers who would visit the service regularly.

We decided that for the pilot project we would get the most full-featured system we could afford so that we could test the different features and determine which ones we needed and which were superfluous. Finally, because the project was a collaboration between many libraries, we did not particularly want a package developed for and focused mainly on ecommerce customer support. A system developed for groups of libraries seemed to us to be the best choice. We determined that 24/7 offered the most features that we wanted to try and met most of our other requirements. The 24/7 licensing was also somewhat flexible and allowed us to negotiate a discount on some elements of the software cost while still configuring the package to meet our needs. The total price, while not the most inexpensive, was manageable when shared among the participating libraries. Each participating library ended up contributing $800 to the project for the pilot year. This cost funded the software, staff training, and promotion of the service.

POLICIES

The service policies were developed by first examining each library's existing reference service policies. Service standards were designed to mimic the service that patrons expected from in-person reference transactions. Policies were drafted to be vague in areas where existing policies relied on the professional judgment of a reference librarian.

The group was more comfortable with the looser guidelines largely because the service was only staffed by reference librarians, not by students or other library staff. If the service had been staffed by non-librarians, more explicit service policies would have been needed. As it was, the guidelines basically set out how to initially respond to a patron request and an ideal "session length"–a suggested amount of time to spend with each patron. The policy also set out what the librarians were *not* supposed to do: provide legal advice or do in-depth research for patrons.

A privacy policy was developed to let patrons know what information we would be gathering from them and what we would and would not do with it. As part of this policy, the group decided not to ask for any personal information that was not needed to provide the service. The task force agreed that requiring users to complete a lengthy form before speaking with a librarian would discourage potential patrons from trying the service.

We required patrons to provide a name or nickname so we could converse with them and required that they pose some sort of question. We asked patrons to provide an e-mail address to receive a transcript of their session and so their librarian could follow up after the real-time session had ended. When the pilot began, we asked for a library affiliation so we would know what resources the patron would have access to if they visited their library in person. This proved confusing to patrons. They believed that by selecting a library they would be connected to someone at that library. To prevent this confusion we stopped asking for library affiliation and determined a patron's "home" library based on the page from which he or she entered the service. When we stopped asking for library affiliation, we began asking for home ZIP code (as an optional field) so that we would be able to determine, generally, where patrons lived. This information was more useful to the public library participants than to the academic partners.

LICENSED RESOURCES

The most difficult policy issue to negotiate among the participants was whether or not to allow librarians to use licensed resources when helping virtual patrons. This actually is too simple a statement of the issue. We largely agreed that a librarian could use a licensed resource to look up an answer and relay it to a patron, just as he or she would use a book. We disagreed on whether or not a page from a licensed resource could be "pushed" or "co-browsed" with a patron. The problems fell into roughly three categories, characterized by questions the librarian would ask about the patron and the resource: "Do you have it?" "Can you have it?" and "May you have it?"

The first question, does the patron have access to the resource, was complicated by the fact that each library had licensed a slightly different menu of resources for its patrons. Many participants had current lists of licensed resources on their web sites, but not all did, and new resources are licensed all the time. Compounding the problem, even if there were a discrete list of all the resources available to a patron of a particular library, some librarians would not be familiar with all of the licensed resources available to a patron of a partner library.

"Can you have it?" is the question that covers the myriad technical problems with trying to share licensed content with remote patrons. The most common form of access to this content was through IP address authentication. Several libraries had CD-ROM materials mounted on local networks. Some libraries still access certain databases using passwords. Each type of resource presented technical access issues. Co-browsing IP-restricted resources was not realistic because of limitations in the service software. Locally mounted resources were not available to Internet users, so librarians could not easily share them with patrons participating in the virtual reference transactions.[1] Password access was less technically problematic, but it raised the very practical question of how to share passwords to half a dozen databases per library among nineteen libraries or forty-odd librarians.

Technical issues notwithstanding, members of the group disagreed on how to read licenses for some resources–the "May you have it" question. While a few licenses clearly prohibited remote access and some clearly allowed it, the majority of them were not clear on this point. In a room full of a dozen law librarians, there were, of course, at least a dozen different interpretations of each license. The various permutations of each license, multiplied by the number of licensed resources, multiplied by the number of libraries, multiplied by the number of patron types, multiplied by the number of librarians trained on each individual database or interface quickly became mind-boggling. In the end, the group decided on a policy that largely left the decision to use licensed resources or not to individual librarians. If the librarian determined that the patron's library had purchased access to an appropriate resource, he or she was comfortable with using that resource, was technically able to access it and felt that the license allowed it to be used, then it could be used.

As it turned out, all of our hand wringing over the licensed resource question was largely unnecessary. Many questions could be answered using freely available web content, much of it developed by the libraries in the normal course of their work. Most librarians were able to help patrons by simply refining their question and pushing a few pages to the patron's screen. Patrons who had more in-depth research needs were referred to their local library (either public law library or large public library) with suggestions for sources and a good research strategy.

TRAINING

Participating librarians met for a day-long training session led by the 24/7 trainer. We held two trainings: one in the southern part of the consortium and one in the northern part. These trainings were hosted by participating libraries and each participating library was required to send at least one librarian to one of the training sessions.

The trainings were held in early summer, with the intention that librarians would have the summer to practice using the software prior to the official launch of the service in the fall. This approach did not work as well as expected because important parts of the training were not fresh in librarians' minds when the service was launched. A training date within a month of the service launch could have reduced this problem.

To help refresh the training and to discuss some service policy issues that arose during the initial phase of the pilot, we held refresher trainings a few months after the service launched. These half-day refresher courses were modeled on the original trainings, but were led by local expert users. Because the librarians had been using the software "in the real world" for a few months, they had specific questions for the trainers and problem solving suggestions for each other. The refresher training sessions proved to be very valuable to the librarians who attended. A significant reduction in the number of technical problems was also noticed after the refresher training.

Because the service is provided by librarians who are geographically dispersed, these meetings allowed for a good exchange of ideas and tips, beyond the formal technical refresher training. The second half of the day at the refresher training meetings was dedicated to discussing the service, policies, problems and how to proceed as the pilot drew to a close. The meetings were also helpful as a training opportunity because librarians were able to suggest solutions to each other.

PROMOTION

Promoting the service was a challenge because we needed to reach many different types of patrons in many different libraries. The group had built some promotion funding into the project's budget, so two series of bookmarks, small posters, and web addresses were developed. The first set of bookmarks had individual libraries' web pages on them, introducing the service and directing patrons to each library's web page to access the service. The second set were developed as a point-of-need reminder that the service was available and gave concrete examples of what patrons could expect when they used the service. Samples of the promotional materials are available on the project web site, www. librarylawline.org.

Posters promoting the service with individual library web addresses were created and distributed electronically to participants for local printing. We created signs for in-person reference desks directing patrons to the service. These are used when a librarian must leave the desk temporarily unattended. This provided a virtual backup librarian for patrons when no local librarian was available, e.g., during staff meetings or while helping another patron away from the desk. The shortcoming of putting posters and signs in libraries is that it does not reach new patrons who may need assistance from a librarian, but are not already in the library. Putting posters or advertisements in places other than the library would help reach this type of patron.

The service web site was created largely for participating librarians to exchange information and coordinate service details, but it also served to promote the service to the public. Early statistics showed that many patrons accessed the service directly from the service web page, as opposed to a specific library's page. (In order to provide more accurate statistics, the service page was changed half way through the pilot to force patrons to choose a library to access the service.)

Each participating library added at last one link to the service from its web page. Many libraries added the service link or a more generic "get help" or "ask a librarian" link to every page in their sites. The libraries whose patrons used the service most heavily prominently displayed links to the service on the front pages of their sites. Some libraries found that placing a general "ask a librarian" or "contact us" link pointing to a detailed reference services page was an effective way to connect patrons to the appropriate reference service offered by the library. For example, on one site, an "ask a librarian" link pointed to a page detailing the virtual reference service, the library's own e-mail reference service, reference desk phone numbers and a postal address. Creating this sort of unified reference services page allows patrons to chose the communication channel they are most comfortable with and which best matches their deadline.

Some academic libraries promoted the service during bibliographic instruction, orientations and library tours. Despite these efforts, academic patrons remained the most difficult to reach. Statistics showed that academic patrons were the least frequent users of the service.

PROBLEMS

One of the most interesting problems faced over the course of the pilot was a fundamental difference in how reference is practiced in public law libraries and academic law libraries. While all of the participating librarians agreed that we could not provide legal advice–practice law– there was a difference in where different libraries drew the boundaries between good reference and practicing law. More fundamental and perhaps more frustrating was the difference in instruction styles between the two different types of library and the concomitant difference in patron expectations. Academic librarians who attempted to do traditional bibliographic instruction were sometimes caught off-guard by a non-law student patron's lack of interest in learning about the research process. Similarly, some patron comments indicated that they expected to get "the answer" from the librarian helping them.

Some librarians who routinely work with lawyers or patrons researching to solve their own legal problems are comfortable suggesting specific form books, search terms, or statutory titles. Conversely, librarians who spend their days teaching the process of legal research to law students seem more likely to view this sort of reference service as providing legal advice or practicing law. This legitimate difference of opinion on what exactly practicing law is and difference in style of providing reference is an area where developing consensus and providing additional training will help improve the service in the future.

As with any complex new electronic service, technical problems were both expected and encountered. Some librarians found that software conflicts on their computers prevented them from using the service altogether. Depending on how much control librarians had over their own computers, some of these issues could be resolved by consulting the vendor's technical support service and fellow librarians who had solved similar problems. One library was unable to resolve the technical issues at all and ended its participation in the pilot early. At least one new software problem developed over the course of the pilot and remained an issue for a few patrons for several months. A new version of the software package resolved the problem.

The group's decision to use a more full-featured software package resulted in more potential for technical issues. It also resulted in a steeper librarian learning curve than we had anticipated. This became a problem when librarians made certain errors that resulted in the service being temporarily unavailable to patrons. These login errors resulted in librarians staffing the service, but being unavailable to patrons, making it seem as if the service was closed when in fact it was not. The mid-year training virtually eliminated this problem, and as librarians become more comfortable with the software, these sorts of issues will be completely resolved.

Even when there were no technical issues or operator error, there were times when the service should have been available but wasn't. Because librarians are human, they occasionally forget–this extends to forgetting to sign on for virtual reference shifts. Again, additional training and policies would reduce this problem. Most software packages, 24/7 included, allow a librarian to see what other librarians are available to answer questions. Implementing a policy that no librarian should exit the service (leave the desk) until the next librarian is properly logged on (at the desk, ready to answer questions) would virtually eliminate this issue. The departing librarian would simply have to call the absent-minded librarian to remind them to sign on–or find out that technical issues like a power outage or building evacuation prevented the librarian from working the shift (as it did at least twice during the NELLCO pilot). An "on call" librarian could then be called on to substitute. Alternatively, a service that always has two librarians scheduled for each shift would be less likely to have two no-shows simultaneously.

Some patrons had questions that could not be easily answered in the chat environment. They required print resources, special databases, or lengthy reading. These patrons still benefited from the service because they were able to work through their question with a subject specialist librarian. Once the librarian determined that the question could not be easily answered, good resources can be suggested and a further plan can be developed. Library LAWLINE patrons were sometimes referred to visit a local library in person; sometimes an e-mail follow up from the original librarian was the best course; sometimes, with the patron's permission, a transcript of the session was forwarded to a local librarian for follow up. By working with a patron to determine the information need, a virtual reference session can provide a good start for research, even if it can't be completed online.

REPORTING AND EVALUATION

Because of the features of the 24/7 software, most reporting was automated. There was some initial work required in order to set up each library's page properly to get patrons into the system and have them counted correctly. Once this set up was complete, the system provided most of the statistics the group was interested in, including patrons by time or day, by library affiliation and by resolution code–entered by the librarian to indicate how the session turned out. Larger consortiums with specialized reporting needs might have to spend time (and money) with the vendor to develop specific reports, but for our needs, the standard reports were sufficient to give us a good picture of how the service was running.

It took a few months for us to realize that allowing patrons to use the service without having visited a library home page first produced problems. First, patrons entering the service from the generic Library LAWLINE promotional page did not always understand that they would be getting help with legal research. Some thought they would be getting free legal advice (we became quite adept at referring patrons to free and low-cost legal service information). More importantly, we had no idea who the patrons were or what library they would be affiliated with. We removed the direct access to the service from the Library LAWLINE page and instead directed patrons to specific library pages where they could access the service. This allowed us to get a better idea of who our patrons were and whether they were our patrons at all. Because several statewide libraries were participants, almost all of our users were within the patron base of at least one of the libraries in the consortium and therefore within the Library LAWLINE patron base.

The group met near the end of the pilot to discuss planning for the future. Though some libraries decided not to continue participating, most acknowledged that some sort of virtual reference is probably in their future. One participant, for example, chose to spend a year providing virtual reference service in conjunction with other libraries on its university campus.

The system reports were used to analyze what hours were most popular as we set a new, somewhat reduced schedule for the service. Because there was very little weekend traffic, and staffing the weekend shifts was the hardest, we eliminated weekend coverage. We kept two librarians available during our busiest hours, which had ten times the traffic of the weekend hours.

We also decided to separate the service into two distinct queues of patrons–one for academic users and one for non-academic users. The task force hoped that this would reduce some of the service problems caused by different expectations of patrons and librarians. The new configuration allows any librarian who wants to participate to determine the type of patron they are willing to help. Many academic librarians will also choose to serve non-academic patrons, but knowing ahead of time that the patron is not a law student should improve the experience for both the librarian and the patron.

As we prepared an evaluation, we found a few significant facts about the service. Law students do not seem to use the service; the general public made up the overwhelming majority of patrons. The busiest hours for the service were from 11:00 a.m. until 3:00 p.m. weekdays. About eight in ten patrons were happy with the service and would use it again. The majority of those who were not pleased cited technical issues or an unmet expectation of getting "the answer" to their question. As determined by question analysis, almost 100% of patrons were within at least one participating library's traditional patron base, but many had never been to their local law library.

Final evaluation of the pilot project is ongoing as this article is being written, but the consensus is that the service will continue with slightly modified hours and the new, two-queue service model. See <http:// www.librarylawline.org> for more information.

RECOMMENDATIONS

Subject-based consortia contemplating setting up a similar service should consider the following lessons learned from the Library LAWLINE pilot: a geographically diverse set of participating libraries will make staffing somewhat easier, doing as much as possible to shape patron expectations before they enter the service will increase patron and librarian satisfaction, an unrestricted number of librarians staffing the systems will make staffing easier and reduce librarian anxiety, and ability to preview or sort questions will result in better service to patrons.

Geographic diversity across time zones will allow early and late staffing of a virtual service without requiring staff to work odd hours or work from home. This is especially valuable in a subject-based consortium because the expertise needed to answer music or medical or legal reference questions is not as dependent on knowledge of local library or collection quirks. The down side to this, as with any shared service, is that staff are less able to answer questions about local library or collection quirks (though this can be remedied somewhat by the use of a FAQ or knowledge-base about local library issues). Library LAWLINE addressed the need for information about particular libraries by having each participant fill in a template of common information and create a saved message in the system that answered frequently asked questions. These saved scripts allowed librarians to quickly answer patron questions about hours, directions, access policies, and services.

Letting patrons know what to expect before they click the "chat" button will help librarians provide better service and help patrons develop more reasonable expectations. In the 24/7 system we used, there are at least two places to put expectation-shaping information. First, on the page that the patron enters the service from, e.g., a reference service page, then on the page where the patron actually fills out the question form. Both of these locations can be used to emphasize what services the librarian can provide. Letting patrons know what the virtual reference librarian can do (help them search a database or suggest a book) and cannot do (in-depth research or document delivery) will help prepare the patron for the online reference interview. In this respect, virtual patrons can have a better idea of what to expect from a librarian than patrons approaching a physical reference desk for the first time.

A service that allows an unlimited number of librarians to be logged in at one time and allows those librarians to preview a question could result in the best available librarian answering the patron inquiry. Policies would need to be developed to ensure that the "hard" questions did not get ignored, but this model, very different from the first-come, first-served model Library LAWLINE uses, would allow many librarians to leave the service running in the background on their computers and screen questions as they come in. Librarians with particular expertise, either about a particular library or in a specific subject area, could select the questions they are best able to answer. A designated, scheduled librarian would then pick up any question not claimed within a certain amount of time.

The NELLCO experience with Library LAWLINE shows that a multi-type subject-based special library consortium can provide a real-time virtual reference service to a diverse patron base. There are obstacles to overcome, but the benefits of providing effective real-time question negotiation to patrons makes overcoming these obstacles worth it. No one model is perfect, but librarians working together can develop services that enhance their service to patrons.

NOTE

1. The 24/7 software allowed librarians to send a screen shot to the patron. This worked well for information that fit onto one screen. If the document was more than one screen, this did not work well.

Planning
for Multilingual Chat Reference Service
in a Suburban Public Library System

Edana McCaffery Cichanowicz
Nan Chen

SUMMARY. Recent immigrants are settling not only in urban centers, but are dispersing throughout the suburban landscape. For many of these new immigrants, the local public library can provide a vital connection to the American Dream, if only librarians can effectively reach them. This article discusses the planning for multilingual chat reference service (currently English, Spanish, and Chinese) and some of the issues and challenges that librarians face in a suburban public library system. *[Article copies available for a fee from The Haworth Document Delivery Service: 1-800-HAWORTH. E-mail address: <docdelivery@haworthpress.com> Website: <http://www.HaworthPress.com> © 2004 by The Haworth Press, Inc. All rights reserved.]*

Edana McCaffery Cichanowicz (E-mail: ecichano@suffolk.lib.ny.us) is Development Coordinator, Reference Service & New Technology, and Nan Chen (E-mail: nchen@suffolk.lib.ny.us) is Catalog/Chinese Service Librarian, both at Suffolk Cooperative Library System, 627 North Sunrise Service Road, Bellport, NY 11713.

The authors' sincere gratitude goes to their Library Administration and colleagues at SCLS for their valuable support and assistance, as well as to the English and Spanish Live Librarians at member libraries for their diligent work. The authors also wish to thank Mei Lee for experimenting with Chinese Live Chat with them.

[Haworth co-indexing entry note]: "Planning for Multilingual Chat Reference Service in a Suburban Public Library System." Cichanowicz, Edana McCaffery, and Nan Chen. Co-published simultaneously in *The Reference Librarian* (The Haworth Information Press, an imprint of The Haworth Press, Inc.) No. 85, 2004, pp. 115-126; and: *Digital versus Non-Digital Reference: Ask a Librarian Online and Offline* (ed: Jessamyn West) The Haworth Information Press, an imprint of The Haworth Press, Inc., 2004, pp. 115-126. Single or multiple copies of this article are available for a fee from The Haworth Document Delivery Service [1-800-HAWORTH, 9:00 a.m. - 5:00 p.m. (EST). E-mail address: docdelivery@haworthpress.com].

KEYWORDS. Live librarian, multilingual chat, public library, Spanish, Chinese, immigrants, multicultural reference service

The modern public library in large measure represents the need of democracy for an enlightened electorate, and its history records its adaptation to changing social requirements.

–Jesse Sheer, *Foundations of the Public Library*

INTRODUCTION

The influx of non-English immigrants arriving in America, in the 19th and early 20th centuries, settled largely in urban centers. They transformed neighborhoods into "Little Italy" or "Chinatown," as they clustered around their local church or temple. City libraries became vital agencies in the successful assimilation of these new Americans, offering them free or affordable recreational, educational opportunities, and support services.

Recent immigrants, however, are settling not only in urban centers, but are dispersing throughout the suburban landscape. For many of these new immigrants, the local public library can still provide a vital connection to the American Dream, if only librarians can effectively reach them.

While these new immigrants are committed to living the American Dream, many are not willing to lose their language and unique ethnic or cultural identity. Some would like their children to be bilingual. Some may prefer services in their native language. Moreover, these preferences may vary from group to group, community to community.

Planning for multilingual chat inevitably positions the library in the midst of a multidimensional intercultural communications challenge. It involves much more than a literal translation of the English-language chat portal, hiring a polyglot staff, and 'getting on with it.' Multilingual chat must reside on a platform of broad-based commitment, by the library, to multicultural sensitivity, service and outreach. The decision to offer multilingual chat reference service inevitably forces the library staff to cope with multicultural issues: how to effectively communicate across significant social and linguistic divides, how to cope with separate but interdependent technical issues, how to implement a portal in each 'in-demand' language, how to decide which languages to 'target,' how to market the service, and how to dovetail the service with existing community programs (such as literacy or citizenship support services). This article will discuss the challenges which arise, as the realization dawns, that multilingual service requires a willingness and ability to think outside of the most basic box of all: our cultural conditioning.

DIMENSIONS OF LOCAL DIVERSITY

Extending an *existing* (English-language) live chat reference service, to include interaction in non-English languages, may seem a relatively simple, even obvious, direction for public libraries to take. Demographics, specifically the 2000 U.S. Census, depict an increasingly diverse suburban population. The 56 public libraries in Suffolk County, New York, serve a multi-ethnic population, lacking in much of the immigrant infrastructure found in a more urban environment. These libraries would be hard-pressed to hire the staff necessary to provide bilingual service in English and one other language, let alone the numerous languages widely spoken in their service areas. One could envision a multilingual chat service as a number of virtual reference service desks, in a variety of languages. While far from perfect, it could provide a shared storefront, for each library, offering at least a commitment to a library presence in the respective linguistic community.

From a practical viewpoint, since the Suffolk project is visualized as extending the English-language service, the first order of business is deciding which languages to branch out into. Should this be based on demographic statistics, community dialog, professional intuition, vocal demand, or a combination of these factors?

The fundamental source of statistical data about languages spoken in U.S. communities is the U.S. Census Bureau. Relevant information includes language spoken at home, ability to speak English, and linguistic isolation. This local data is most easily accessible via the U.S. Census pathfinder at <http://factfinder.census.gov/>.

While the census provides fundamental data, it is only a part of the overall picture. What groups in the community identify themselves as unable to cope with English without assistance? This data is most likely available from local literacy advocacy groups, educational institutions, and social support agencies, which can assist librarians in determining the relative numbers of group members seeking instruction in English as a Second Language and Basic Literacy. Literacy Volunteers of America/Suffolk provides the best local data for Suffolk County: the ESL program is populated by (as determined from a sample of recent applicants), in descending order, native speakers of: Spanish, Chinese, Korean, Turkish, and Polish. This list provides additional insight into evaluating the degree of local need for multilingual assistance.

As a cooperative system, our member libraries' wishes are most persuasive. One member, because of a large and influential Portuguese community, has expressed an interest in including such service in our future planning. Anecdotally, we determined from numerous library visits that the demand for Chinese and Korean is overwhelming, as was borne out by the literacy statistics. Establishing a meaningful dialogue among various service agencies and constituencies is critical.

The practicalities of staff recruitment likewise enter into the picture. What fluencies are extant in available staff? Our current chat reference staff is fluent in English, Spanish, Chinese, German, and Russian. We may turn to local academic institutions, to recruit from an international employment pool. Diversity must extend, in the short and long term, to appropriate staff recruitment. A diversified workforce would obviously help address the necessity for diversified services.

Suffolk County, given the realities of local demographics, statistics on enrollment in literacy programs, and staff expertise, decided to begin the expansion of live chat reference service into Chinese and Spanish.

THE PORTAL ISSUE

The placement and accessibility of the entry-level web page, and its content, are of critical importance. We are in the content business, whether it's offering information about library collections via the OPAC, links to web sites, or subscription databases in a variety of languages. Ideally, all of these elements will converge at the portal.

Intuition tells us that the portal should function as welcoming signage, that it should be of maximum accessibility, and that it should provide rich content on culturally significant topics.

Constructing such an entrée is relatively simple, in a European or alphabetic language. The libraries in Suffolk County subscribe to a number of Spanish language databases, including the Gale Group's *¡Informe!* and Newsbank's *Notícias*, several libraries have Spanish language web sites, and there is a rudimentary Spanish language page for those without the resources to develop a customized page for their library. There are also Chinese and Portuguese pages, but no subscription databases (yet) in these languages. Within our member libraries patrons will find a variety of books, periodicals, newspapers, videos, DVDs, and audiocassettes in the target languages. They may see some friendly signage, pointing out areas or collections of special interest. However, these patrons will, for the most part, encounter librarians who speak English and only English. This presents a problem in communicating the information of most critical interest to our target groups: how to find English as a Second Language (ESL) classes, how to locate ESL materials in the catalog, where to find reliable information about immigration, social security, employment, and a 'welcome to your library' message. Presenting a basic web portal for some of this material, in Spanish or another European language, is relatively simple, as long as we stay focused on practical service. *How long can I keep a video out? Are library fines reported to the authorities? Do I need a green card to get a library card? Can I really borrow free audiocassettes? Do you have free English classes here? How do I know when you have story hours for children? What sort of identification do I need to become a borrower?* FAQs, as much as we love to hate them, are not a tremendous issue in European/alphabetic languages. Adding Spanish reference chat is, relatively speaking, a simple goal for Suffolk libraries. We have a rudimentary collection, a number of bilingual librarians, and flexible chat software. We also coordinate, through the auspices of Instituto Cervantes, formal classes in *Spanish for Library Workers*. While the latter will not instantly create bilingual librarians, it provides an entrée to librarians interested in mastering conversational Spanish, trains staff in expressing the courtesies in a second language, and demonstrates that public service staff in Suffolk county libraries are anxious to overcome the inertia that keeps each group locked in linguistic isolation.

Creating a web page in a pictographic language, such as Chinese, presents new challenges and questions, however. Should the page be written in Simplified or Traditional font? How will each display? What are the problems, if any, in choosing one, over another? Perhaps the most courteous route is to create a Chinese page that includes both fonts, since this will avoid presuming a political orientation. Simplified characters are used in the People's Republic, Traditional characters in Taiwan and Hong Kong. If the page combines both, and they are displayed as graphical elements such as gifs, there is no need for the immediate intrusion of error messages, such as 'Do you want to install this font now? If so insert the CD.' First things first, create a page that displays characters passively, on both library in-house computers, for patrons and for remote users.

TRAINING AND TECHNICAL CONSIDERATIONS

Successful deployment requires negotiating a number of separate but interrelated technical issues. Browsers support a nearly endless variety of fonts, but they must be installed, a question of staff training, and technical support, within the libraries. Many patrons, from the target language groups, have demonstrated that they know more than the average Anglo librarian about fonts, keyboards, and displaying multilingual text.

As to chat software, when online, the chat software must support the target languages, from librarian and patron end. If off-line e-mail is accepted, that software must also support the target languages. If the librarian will be composing messages, s/he may need the appropriate word processing program. Finally, if the patron receives an e-mail message in response, s/he may also need the appropriate software, in order to read it. Commercial software has been internationalized, to cover these eventualities, to varying degrees. The best way to determine what works most effectively on your system is to test, test, and re-test. This became, for us, an exercise in 'avoiding gibberish.'

LIVE CHAT IN CHINESE–
SOME TECH ASPECTS IN A NUTSHELL

How to Display Chinese Characters on the Screen

We downloaded Simplified and Traditional fonts from Yahoo. Both fonts are needed because some web sites are in Simplified characters and some are in Traditional ones, while some web sites employ gifs to make sure that the page display properly displays, without the user needing to install anything.

How to Input Chinese Characters

You do not need a special Chinese keyboard. An English word processor, such as Microsoft Word, and a Chinese word processor will do. This is important. In our experience, the fonts downloaded from the Internet only allow us to *display* the existing texts in Chinese web sites, while a Chinese word processor makes it possible for us to *input* Chinese characters in a document.

The Chinese word processor we installed is called Chinese Star. Using a regular English keyboard, we are able to "type" Chinese characters on the screen by using Pinyin, a phonetic system that converts the sounds into the words (characters). For example, ni → 你 = you, hao → 好 = good, together "ni hao" 你好 = Hello or How are you?

How to Select a Chinese Word Processor

There are a number of Chinese word processors available on the market, such as NJStar, ChineseStar, Twin Bridge, etc., currently costing from $99 to $300 depending on the level of capacity. They come in different versions compatible with different Windows versions, such as Windows 95/98, or Windows 2000/XP/NT. Among other things, a good Chinese word processor should allow you to input either Simplified or Traditional characters at your choice.

Simplified vs. Traditional Characters

It is felt that some basic background information about the Chinese language is needed here in order for the reader to better understand the challenges we are facing with the Chinese online services.

As the name implies, Simplified characters have fewer strokes than the Traditional ones, for example, 图书馆 vs. 圖書館 = Library, pronounce as "tu shu guan" (Pinyin). The pronunciation is the same for Simplified and Traditional characters (tu = picture, shu = book, guan = house, together "tu shu guan" = picture book house = library).

Traditional Chinese characters date back to about 3,500 years ago. Although the largest Chinese dictionary contains more than 50,000 characters, only 3,000-4,000 are needed for day-to-day use.

In the 1950s, Mainland China decided to simplify some of the commonly used characters in the effort to make learning and writing the language easier.

Today, Simplified characters are used in Mainland China, Singapore, and overseas Chinese communities, while Traditional characters are used in Taiwan, Hong Kong, as well as overseas Chinese communities.

Pinyin

Unlike Western languages, Chinese characters are pictographic and independent from their sounds. In 1958, a phonetic system called Pinyin was devised in Mainland in order not only to serve as a learning bridge between the sounds and the characters but also to standardize spelling of

Chinese in Western languages. At school, children learn Pinyin (the sound) first, then learn to read and write the characters with the help of Pinyin, and, finally, Pinyin is dropped from the textbook as children have learned a sufficient number of characters.

Pinyin has been recognized by the International Standards Organization (ISO), the United Nations, the U.S. government, and Library of Congress. Now almost all the Chinese language records in OCLC have been converted from Wade-Giles romanization system to Pinyin. 'Peking' has since become 'Beijing,' 'Szechwan' has become 'Sichuan,' and 'Canton' has become 'Guangdong,' to name a few.

Mandarin vs. Cantonese

People are often confused between Mandarin and Cantonese, or between them and Chinese characters.

Mandarin and Cantonese are spoken languages or dialects. Chinese characters are written language.

Mandarin, based on Beijing dialect, is the official language spoken by the majority of the entire Chinese population and is used on TV, radio and in movies in Mainland and Taiwan. On the other hand, Cantonese is a Chinese dialect spoken in Guangdong (Canton) Province and Hong Kong only. The reason that Cantonese dialect is much more prevalent than Mandarin in Chinatowns throughout the United States is that during the 19th and early 20th centuries the majority of the Chinese immigrants who came to the U.S. were from the Guangdong area because of its proximity to the Pacific Ocean. Hong Kong used to be part of Guangdong before it became a colony of Britain over 100 years ago. In 1997, Hong Kong was returned to China and is now a "Special Administrative Region" under PRC.

Therefore, references to spoken Chinese, without any qualification, are usually to Mandarin.

As far as written Chinese is concerned, even though there are more than 50 dialects spoken in Mainland China and Taiwan, there is virtually only one written system, with the exception of Simplified characters and Traditional characters within the system. Books and newspapers published in Mainland are in Simplified characters and those in Taiwan are in Traditional characters. What about those published in the United States? They are in both characters. As mentioned earlier, the pronunciations of the characters are the same. Many Chinese can read both because not all the Traditional characters are being simplified. For example:

雅虎 (yahoo) looks the same in Simplified and Traditional scripts. In literal translation, 雅 ya = elegant, 虎 hu = tiger, go figure, 'yahoo' in Chinese stands for 'Elegant Tiger.' How's that?

CONCLUSIONS

1. Choose service needs over 'rational' technical limitations. While it's vital to engage the technical staff in a meaningful dialogue, one can't allow technical considerations alone to drive the service agenda. As the practical patron needs became focused on Spanish and Chinese, we knew that we were going to be forced to deal with a plethora of very complex technical issues: non-English display and keyboarding, staffing, collection development, to name three of the most prominent. We truly didn't forsee many of the new problems created by solving one problem. If we had, discretion might have prevailed, and we would never have gotten as far as we have.
2. Don't be afraid to fail. Experiment. We learn more from our failures than our success.
3. Keep a sense of perspective:

   Chat is not a substitute for face-to-face reference.
   Chat is interactive signage.
   Chat is an attempt at outreach.
   Chat is an alternative approach.
   Chat shows we are, at least, trying.
   Chat may fill some of the needs, of some of our patrons, some of the time.
   Chat is not perfect, but it doesn't have to be; nothing else we do is perfect.

4. Translation is not synonymous with communication. Keep it simple. Cut as much tit-for-tat literal translation of library jargon as you can. Stay focused on WHAT you are trying to communicate.
5. "Other" cultural groups are not monolithic, but contain their own intragroup diversity. Second and third generation Latinos have slightly different agendas, for example, than newly arrived immigrants. Understand and enjoy this diversity within diversity!

REFERENCES

Academic American Encyclopedia. Grolier Inc. 1998.

Barnes, Louis B., C. Roland Christensen and Abby J. Hansen. *Teaching and the Case Method.* Boston, Massachusetts. Harvard Business School Press. 1994.

Blandy, Susan Griswold. "What to Do Until the Expert Comes: Dealing with Demands for Multicultural, International Information Now." *The Reference Librarian* no. 45-46 (1994) p. 119-35.

Brake, Terence, Danielle Medina Walker and Thomas (Tim) Walker. *Doing Business Internationally: The Guide to Cross-cultural Success.* Boston, Massachusetts. McGraw-Hill. 1995.

Brown, Christopher C. "Reference Services to the International Adult Learner: Understanding the Barriers." *The Reference Librarian* no. 69-70 (2000) p. 337-47.

Chattoo, Calmer D. "Reference Services: Meeting the Needs of International Adult Learners." *The Reference Librarian* no. 69-70 (2000) p. 349-62.

Childers, Thomas. "Using Public Library Reference Collections and Staff." *The Library Quarterly* v. 67 (April 1997) p. 155-73.

Clara M. Chu. "Education for Multicultural Librarianship" In: *Multiculturalism in Libraries,* Edited by Rosemary Ruhig Du Mont, Lois Buttlar, and William Caynon. Westport, CT: Greenwood Press, 1994; p. 127-56.

Foley, May. "Reference and Information Services in a Multi-cultural Environment." *Journal of Library and Information Science (Taipei, Taiwan)* v. 10 (October 1984) p. 143-62.

Hall, Edward T. and Mildred Reed Hall. *Understanding Cultural Differences.* Yarmouth, Maine. Intercultural Press. 1990.

Judd, Blanche E., Michael J. McLane and Nancy Seale Osborne. "Valuing Diversity: Students Helping Students." *The Reference Librarian* no. 45-46 (1994) p. 93-110.

Liestman, Daniel. "Reference Services and the International Adult Learner." *The Reference Librarian* no. 69-70 (2000) p. 363-78.

Manley, Will. "Multiculturalism or Gender Equity?" *American Libraries* v. 28 (June/July 1997) p. 160.

Neely, Teresa Y. "Ethnic Colorado." *Colorado Libraries* v. 21 (Summer 1995) p. 4-38.

Samovar, Larry A. and Richard E. Porter. *Intercultural Communication: A Reader.* Belmont, California. Wadsworth Publishing. 2000.

Stephen Stern. "Ethnic Libraries and Librarianship in the United States: Models and Prospects."*Advances in Librarianship* 15 (1991) p. 77-102.

Winston, Mark D. "Cultural Sensitivity; or, How to Make the Library a Better Place." *Reference Services Review* v. 23 no. 3 (1995) p. 7-12.

APPENDIX

CHINESE PHP LIVE CHAT SCREEN SAMPLE

(Traditional characters)

Chat Transcript - Microsoft Internet Explorer   `_ □ ×`

"Chinese chat 中文線上參考服務"

** You are now speaking with **Chinese Live Librarian, chinese**. **

Mei : 你好!, 我已上線

Chinese Live Librarian : 梅，你好，

Mei : 收到信息了

Mei : 你可以和我一起co-browsing嗎

Chinese Live Librarian : 很高興，我想可以

Mei : 可以試播google的網頁給我嗎

Chinese Live Librarian : 中文還是英文？

Mei : 都可以

Chinese Live Librarian : 請稍候。

Mei : 我目前在用台灣國家圖書館的遠距圖書服務系統, 網址為 http://readopac.ncl.edu.tw/, 也賊y後你可以也試試

Chinese Live Librarian : 假如我們斷了線，我會再回來，

Mei : ok

APPENDIX (continued)

SAMPLE OF MULTILINGUAL CANNED RESPONSES

English	Spanish	Chinese
Hi, How may we help you?	*¡Hola! ¿Como puedo ayudarle?*	你好，請問你有什麼問題？
OK. Please hold on while I look for that.	*OK. Por favor no cuelgue. Estoy buscando su informacíon.*	請稍候。
I will push a web page to your computer.	*Empujaré una página directamente a su computatdora.*	我傳一個網頁給你。
I have e-mailed some information to you.	*Se le mandé información por correo electrónico.*	我已 e-mail 給你一些資料。
Does that completely answer your question?	*¿Hemos respondidos completamente a su pregunta?*	答案滿意嗎？
Thank you for using Live Librarian.	*Gracias para usar este servicio Adiós.*	謝謝使用網上服務。

SECTION THREE:
A FEW THINGS TO THINK ABOUT

The Social Life of Digital Reference:
What the Technology Affords

Mita Sen-Roy

SUMMARY. Digital reference service (also known as virtual reference) has become a contentious topic in the library literature, as some critics feel that it threatens reference service more than it enhances it. Through this paper it is hoped that the debate can be refocused after a careful assessment of what exactly digital reference technology can *afford* and what social impact such affordances could bring. The suggestion will be made that digital reference should be employed as a means to provide reference service as long as the service is designed to play to the strengths of the technology. As such, it is recommended that libraries

Mita Sen-Roy is Science Librarian, Leddy Library, University of Windsor, Ontario, Canada, N9B 3P4 (E-mail: msenroy@uwindsor.ca).

[Haworth co-indexing entry note]: "The Social Life of Digital Reference: What the Technology Affords." Sen-Roy, Mita. Co-published simultaneously in *The Reference Librarian* (The Haworth Information Press, an imprint of The Haworth Press, Inc.) No. 85, 2004, pp. 127-137; and: *Digital versus Non-Digital Reference: Ask a Librarian Online and Offline* (ed: Jessamyn West) The Haworth Information Press, an imprint of The Haworth Press, Inc., 2004, pp. 127-137. Single or multiple copies of this article are available for a fee from The Haworth Document Delivery Service [1-800-HAWORTH, 9:00 a.m. - 5:00 p.m. (EST). E-mail address: docdelivery@haworthpress.com].

pursue digital reference service that is local, professional, and with privacy constraints. *[Article copies available for a fee from The Haworth Document Delivery Service: 1-800-HAWORTH. E-mail address: <docdelivery@ haworthpress.com> Website: <http://www.HaworthPress.com> © 2004 by The Haworth Press, Inc. All rights reserved.]*

KEYWORDS. Digital reference, virtual reference, reference service, affordance

INTRODUCTION

Digital reference has become a contentious topic in the library literature. On one side it's "virtual reference: overrated, inflated, and not even real"[1] and on the other, it is deemed a critical necessity otherwise reference librarians "will become extinct."[2] At these extremes, those who advocate the use of e-mail or 'chat' reference service imply that such action should be deemed critical, citing recent ARL[3] and Pew Internet and American Life reports.[4] Those in the library literature critical of digital reference voice a strong rebuff, claiming that digital reference promotes different values than are inherent in traditional walk-in, in-person reference help[5] and may even threaten these values.[6]

The suggestion that a change of medium can fundamentally change the human values expressed through traditional desk reference service reveals an understanding that no technology is neutral. This is not a point of view shared by everyone and so it deserves further explanation. Langdon Winner does this eloquently in his book *The Whale and the Reactor: A Search for Limits in an Age of High Technology*. He writes:

> The language of the notion of "use" also includes standard terms that enable us to interpret technologies in a range of moral contexts. Tools can be "used well or poorly" and for "good or bad purposes"; I can use my knife to slice a loaf of bread or to stab the next person that walks by. Because technological objects and processes have a promiscuous utility, they are taken to be fundamentally neutral as regards to their moral standing . . .

But, as Winner goes on to say:

> If the experience of modern society shows us anything, however, it is that technologies are not merely aids to human activity, but also

powerful forces acting to reshape that activity and its meaning. The introduction of a robot to an industrial workplace not only increases productivity but often radically changes the process of production, redefining what "work" means in that setting. When a sophisticated new technique or instrument is introduced in medical practice, it transforms only what doctors do, but also the ways people think about health, sickness, and medical care.

As such, it is important to evaluate our choices of technology as measured by their potential social impact. "From this point of view, the important question about technology becomes, As we 'make things work,' what kind of *world* are we making?"[7] What kind of world is made by the employment of digital reference service? How does this technology reshape human activity in the library? These are important questions to raise now as digital reference technology is still in a nascent stage of development.

Not only is it useful to examine the sort of abilities and possibilities that digital reference technology possesses but exactly what this technology can *afford*. The concept of affordance in the digital realm has been employed most notably by Don Norman.[8] Following his lead, a number of librarians have used the concept of affordability as a means to improve usability of library web sites.[9,10]

The concept of affordances originates in psychology:

> The notion of affordances can be traced to the ecological psychologist J. J. Gibson in his seminal book *The Ecological Approach to Visual Perception*. Gibson's theory was that people "pick up" information about their environment and the objects in it largely by attending to what those objects afford. An affordance refers to the fact that the physical properties of an object make possible different functions for the person perceiving or using that object.[11]

An examination of a technology's affordances can be quite enlightening. By examining the affordances of paper and careful study of how paper and computers are actually used in the workplace, Sellen and Harper explain why the advent of computers has led to an *increase* of paper use and not a paperless office. Their research suggests that paper possesses significant advantages over computers by the way that paper affords better conditions for collaborative work.

Following Sellen and Harper's example, this paper seeks a better grasp of what human activities can be supported by digital reference service and for which activities it is should be employed with reservations. In addressing the most significant affordances of digital reference software, no particular brand of software will be addressed but only a generalization of the currently existing software. It will be assumed that the reader is already familiar with digital reference technology. If not, the works suggested in Bernie Sloan's Digital Reference Primer[12] is a recommended starting point for these readers.

THE AFFORDANCE OF VISIBILITY

Some libraries offer digital reference service at the reference desk. This scenario can be used to highlight one difference in affordance between traditional reference service and that of digital reference service: the affordance of visually conveying activity to others. A library user approaching the reference desk can see if the librarian is currently speaking with another library user and hear the nature of the conversation. A library user approaching the reference desk can see if the librarian is on the phone with another library user and also hear the nature of the conversation. But if a library user approaching the reference desk with a librarian typing at a computer, this user has no way of knowing whether the librarian is writing a document (which some users would feel comfortable interrupting) or engaging in a 'chat' and assisting an off-site library user. A librarian engaged in a digital reference interaction at the reference desk who is approached at the desk by a library user seeking assistance has the choice of asking the in-library user to wait or ask the out-of-library user engaged in chat to be placed on hold. Because the in-library user is unable to discern that the librarian is engaged in an online chat that is not merely social, the librarian may feel it necessary to explain that she is currently helping another user. Because digital reference does not afford the ability to convey to other users its activity, a number of libraries have decided to provide digital reference service through service points other than the reference desk.

THE AFFORDANCE OF CONTENT

The most common alternative to traditional face-to-face reference service is that of reference service facilitated by the telephone. Phone reference service is more widely available to library users as the phone network is the largest in human history.[5] But unlike the phone, digital reference affords digital documents and links to documents to be easily and immediately exchanged. Not only is a librarian able to send any digital document on hand, it is possible for the librarian to send digital artifacts such as sound files, video clips, or multimedia. Bandwidth may be an issue if the documents in question are exceptionally large, but the distance between collection and library user is no longer a barrier if that collection has been digitized. Content within the library that has not been digitized must be accessed within the library; a librarian offering digital reference service can only offer the library catalogue record of a non-digitized item or digitized supporting documents.

At the risk of over-generalizing the findings of Sellen and Harper, digital documents afford superior storage, searching, and retrieval whereas print documents afford better reading, marking up, and collaborative work. To the out-of-library user, this means that digital documents are more convenient to retrieve than the printed material that requires a trip to the library. Consequently, librarians who provide digital reference service should consider how they will present potential information sources to library users. Should a librarian only present the most appropriate source to a query or is a librarian obliged to provide the most convenient source as well? Or as Thomas Mann asks the question, "To what extent can librarians—surrounded by copyrighted print sources, and by the vast bulk of public domain print sources that are too expensive to digitize, and by site-licensed databases that are not freely available in cyberspace—provide reference service to remote users who are not inside the walls?"[13] Mann considers digital reference services to off-site library users an unfortunate "tradeoff" that threatens to devalue the print collections of libraries and in doing so, threatens the value of the library itself. Others, such as Anne Lipnow, see the digital reference service as an opportunity that must be taken so librarians can promote the print collection of the library:

> If we do not begin now to demonstrate the need for reference librarians by providing service that recognizes our clientele's new ways of searching for information, there is more at stake than reference service by reference librarians. First, by our inaction, we contribute to the decline in the use of the library's print materials. Online commercial information services draw entirely on electronic sources . . . The information seeker using one of these commercial services will never get the response 'The question you are asking is better handled by a wonderful reference book that is available in your library.'[2]

Further discussion of this issue of appropriateness versus convenience and how librarians may be able to influence students' web-based information choices[14] can be found in the library literature.

THE AFFORDANCE TO TRANSCEND GEOGRAPHY

As digital reference requires a computer network to connect the librarian with the library user, the geographical area that can be served by digital reference is dependent only on the availability of access to the network. This means that the library user can be anywhere: in the next continent or the next room over. Both scenarios are likely in an academic library: many universities are providing distance education programs and promoting such services overseas and it has already been documented that some users within libraries make use of digital reference service so as not to lose their seat at a public computer.[15] Digital reference service may even be preferred to phone reference service to those library users who are so far from the library that "long-distance" phone rates apply as Internet access is charged by a set fee, by time used, by bytes downloaded, or a combination of these options.

With no physical barriers to worry about, the library user effectively has more choice in which library to approach for reference help. How does a library user decide when to visit the web site of her local library rather than the nearest university library, national library, or some other library of renown? It's not known–there hasn't been much research in the descriptions of information-seeking behaviour in an online environment.[15]

What *is* known is that when an offsite library user visits the web site of a library that is not "her own," she will not have access to that library's online proprietary databases. The affordances that make digital documents easy to transmit are also the same qualities that allow digital documents to be easily copied and shared. The social constraint of copyright legislation has been established so that proliferation of proprietary materials does not become rampant. Consequently, libraries have established validation systems to ensure that online access to digital collections of publications are restricted to only the members of libraries as required by publishers' licensing agreements, the ramification of which is that, as access to digital documents is concerned, the library does not care where you are but *who* you are. This is significantly different from how libraries handle the copyright restrictions of printed material. Most libraries allow all members of the public to browse the books of their collection. "They can provide *free* access to copyrighted print sources, especially books . . . because libraries impose on them a *where* restriction to a place within walls."[16]

Not only can the library user be outside of the library when engaged in digital reference service, it is possible that a librarian can be physically located outside of the library as well. This model has been most notably expounded by Steve Coffman who suggests that libraries would be wise to emulate customer call centers as a means to maximize the efficiency of reference librarians.[17] Juris Dilevko strenuously opposes the call center model and suggests that such a move will lead to deprofessionalization of those involved.[6] Deskilling is also an issue. Placing librarians outside of the library building or mandating that a librarian only perform digital reference service effectively ensures that the librarians' knowledge of a library's print collection will diminish over time.

One could argue that the primary reason why the call center model of digital reference service has been pursued is due to the fact that a call center is cheaper to maintain than a library, especially if the goal is to provide 24/7 digital reference service for a library's 24/7 digital reference collection or to "compete with the Internet." Some libraries are pursuing this same goal but not by means of call centers; these libraries are partnering with other libraries–some in other time zones–to expand hours of digital reference service. These libraries are taking advantage of the affordances of digital communication to allow for collaborative work over large distances. "And all these examples of interconnection and independence are the result of our being poor. Let's face the truth–if libraries as a group were better funded and supported, it's quite likely that some of these examples of sharing would not exist or be far less extensive."[18]

THE AFFORDANCE OF WORKING ALONE

Research in the library is generally considered a solitary activity. Brown and Duguid explain the distinctions of learning in solitary and social environments by contrasting the car and the VCR:

> Almost everyone in our society who learns to drive has already spent a great deal of time traveling in cars or buses, along roads and highways. New drivers begin formal instruction with an implicitly structured, social understanding of the task. Now consider the VCR. Most people can use their machines to play tapes. What

they find more difficult is recording although that's not a much more complex task. The central distinction between these two functions is that one is often a social act, the other is highly individual.[19]

But research within the library isn't a completely solitary endeavor. In their work, "Browsing Is a Collaborative Process," Twidale, Nichols, and Paice documented significant social interaction within the library as library users sought out how to use the library system from friends, strangers, staff, and librarians. Even those users who do not actively engage other library users can watch and see how others in the building are acting and can try to learn from what they see.

The digitized library environment completely lacks these visual cues. As such, it is feared that

> any trend towards remote searching will make traditional collaborative interactions rarer by losing physical proximity to other searchers. Even today, access from one's own room to the local online public access catalogue (OPAC) system is reducing the opportunities for social interaction, and with the development of full-blown digital libraries this tendency will be intensified.[20]

One of the most common points brought up by advocates of digital reference service is that the technology provides ability for the librarian to be available at the point-of-need–online with the library user. How digital reference service may be applied as a means to support the library user of the digital library has been explored in the library literature.[21]

THE AFFORDANCE OF PRIVACY AND LACK OF PRIVACY

Michael Gorman has formulated a shortlist of fundamentals that he feels should inform librarianship. One of these eight values is privacy.

> Users of reference services are entitled to privacy. This presents a particular problem. Most libraries seek to make reference areas open and welcoming, but those digital are inimical to privacy. This can be a real problem in dealing with "sensitive" subjects or with shy, easily intimidated library users.[5]

In this context, one could make the case that digital reference service can provide a more comfortable venue for shy patrons or those embarrassed. For example, digital reference service may be preferred by those students who know English as a second language and feel more comfortable with their written skills than with their verbal abilities. I also suspect that library users who wish to conceal ignorance or need, such as faculty members in an academic library setting, may also enjoy the ability to ask questions of the library anonymously.

But the ability to use digital reference service anonymously is not an inherent aspect of digital reference. Many libraries require users of digital reference service to fill out forms before an online chat can be initiated. These forms ask the user to self-identify asking for (in frequency of order given) name, e-mail address, phone number, affiliation, mailing address, fax number, and deadline.[22] We do not ask our walk-in patrons to self identify before they ask us a question, why do we require it of our online users? In the age of the U.S. PATRIOT Act, libraries should seriously rethink such policies or destroy information that can be used to identify the library user.

The privacy rights of librarians should also be seriously considered when a digital reference is employed as digital media affords the possibility of monitoring computer activity right down to the keystroke. Currently, most brands of digital reference software are unconcerned with what librarians do when not answering digital reference questions but do save and store the transcript of very digital reference transactions. Anecdotal evidence has suggested these transcripts may prove useful learning tools and a fruitful ground for future research.[23] Intellectual property concerns may also be raised in the future if these transactions are mined for the marketing of "reusable reference objects."[18]

CONCLUSION: OUR STRENGTH IS SOCIAL

As reference librarians we understand that what our users ask for isn't always what they want. In many instances, the user does not know who collects and publishes the information that they are interested in. "Whether consciously aware of it or not, when anybody asks us a question, the first thing we (librarians) do is sort through our mental maps of the information territory."[24]

Reference librarians are better positioned than most to understand this social context of information and the importance of people in knowledge transfer and information distribution. Libraries serve as both social and knowledge intermediaries every day.[25]

Information is created in a social context and the delivery of information through digital media does not change this. Digital reference can be employed as a means to provide a human presence in an online environment to assist users at a point of need and to make librarians' work less invisible.[2] Such a service will allow us to extend our traditional role as information intermediaries into an online environment. The long-term success of digital reference service–especially the collaborative digital reference projects that are presently in their beginning stages–will greatly depend on whether the services will play into the strengths of what the technology can afford. As such, it is recommended that libraries pursue digital reference service that is local, professional, and with privacy constraints.

ENDNOTES

1. "Virtual Reference: Overrated, Inflated, and Not Even Real." <http://www.charlestonco.com/features.cfm?id=112&type=ed> April 14.

2. "Serving the Remote User: Reference Service in the Digital Environment. Keynote Address at the Ninth Australasian Information Online & On Disc Conference and Exhibition in Sydney, Australia." <http://www.csu.edu.au/special/online99/proceedings99/200.htm/> April 14.

3. Association of Research Libraries (ARL). "ARL statistics, 2000-01." <http://www.arl.org/arl/pr/statistics2000-01.html> April 14.

4. Pew Internet & American Life Project. "Counting on the Internet." <http://www.pewinternet.org/reports/pdfs/PIP_Expectations.pdf> April 14.

5. Gorman, Michael. "Values for Human-to-Human Reference." *Library Trends* 50 (Fall 2001): 168-182.

6. Dilevko, Juris. "An Ideological Analysis of Digital Reference Service Models." *Library Trends* 50 (Fall 2001): 218-244.

7. Winner, Langdon. *The Whale and the Reactor: A Search for Limits in an Age of High Technology.* Chicago: University of Chicago Press, 1989.

8. Norman, Donald A. *Design of Everyday Things.* New York: Doubleday, 1990.

9. "The Third Wave of the Information Age: Internet Librarian Conference November 2001." <http://www.infotoday.com/searcher/feb02/mcdermott.htm>.

10. "The User is the Expert: Experiences at Three Universities Using Usability Studies to Inform Gateway and Tutorial Web Designs, ACRL 9th National Conference." <http://www.tc.umn.edu/~jveldof/ACRL99/userdesign.html> April 14.

11. Sellen, Abigail J., and Harper, Richard H. R. *The Myth of the Paperless Office.* Cambridge, Massachusetts: The MIT Press, 2002.

12. "Digital Reference Primer." <http://www.lis.uiuc.edu/~b-sloan/primer.htm> April 14, 2003.

13. Mann, Thomas. "Reference Service, Human Nature, Copyright, and Offsite Service–in a 'Digital Age.' " *Reference & User Services Quarterly* 38 (1998): 55-61.

14. "How Academic Librarians can Influence Students' Web-Based Information Choices." <http://www2.oclc.org/oclc/pdf/printondemand/informationhabits.pdf> April 14.

15. Francoeur, Stephen. "An Analytical Survey of Chat Reference Service." *Reference Services Review* 29 (2001): 189-203.

16. Mann, Thomas. "The Importance of Books, Free Access, and Libraries as Places–and the Dangerous Inadequacy of the Information Science Paradigm." *The Journal of Academic Librarianship* 27 (July 2001): 268-281.

17. Coffman, Steve. "Reference As Others Do It." *American Libraries* 30 (1999): 54-56.

18. Janes, Joseph. "Why Reference Is About to Change Forever (but Not Completely)." In *Digital Reference Service in the New Millennium: Planning, Management, and Evaluation*, edited by R. David Lankes John W. Collins and Abby S. Kasowitz. New York: Neal-Schuman Publishers, 2000.

19. Brown, John Seely, and Duguid, Paul. *The Social Life of Information.* Boston, Massachusetts: Harvard Business School Press, 2000.

20. "Browsing is a Collaborative Process." <http://www.comp.lancs.ac.uk/computing/research/cseg/projects/ariadne/docs/bcp.html> April 14.

21. Sloan, Bernie. "Service Perspectives for the Digital Library: Remote Reference Services." *Library Trends* 47 (Summer 1998): 117-143.

22. Janes, Joseph, and Silverstein, Joanne. "Question Negotiation and the Technological Environment." *D-Lib Magazine* 9 (February 2003).

23. Tennant, Roy. "Revisiting Digital Reference." *Library Journal* 128 (January 2003): 38, 40.

24. Block, Marylaine. "My Rules of Information." *Searcher* 10 (January 2002).

25. Fritch, John W., and Mandernack, Scott B. "The Emerging Reference Paradigm: A Vision of Reference Services in a Complex Information Environment." *Library Trends* 50 (Fall 2001): 286-305.

The Case for Non-Intrusive Research: A Virtual Reference Librarian's Perspective

Bruce Jensen

SUMMARY. Electronic reference facilitates analyses not possible in face-to-face and telephone transactions. Texts of e-mail and chat reference sessions disambiguate issues of accuracy, interview discourse, and, to a lesser extent, patron satisfaction. Authentic transcripts are here advanced as superior instruments for study of AskA services, with significant applications also in better understanding other modes of reference. Clandestine questioning by colleagues, MLIS students, and researchers afflicts online reference services; it is argued here that unobtrusive study techniques useful in traditional settings are inappropriate for online reference, generating dubious data while undermining service quality. This paper examines how research affects the work of virtual reference librarians, and suggests appropriate means of assessing virtual reference services for scholarly as well as library management purposes. *[Article copies available for a fee from The Haworth Document Delivery Service: 1-800-HAWORTH. E-mail address: <docdelivery@haworthpress.com> Website: <http://www. HaworthPress.com> © 2004 by The Haworth Press, Inc. All rights reserved.]*

KEYWORDS. Action research, assessment, corpus analysis, evaluation, reference, electronic reference, chat reference, research methods, methodology/methodologies, transcripts, virtual reference

---

Bruce Jensen is Reference Librarian, Metropolitan Cooperative Library System, 3675 East Huntington Drive, Suite 100, Pasadena, CA 91107-5671 (E-mail: flaco@sol-plus.net).

[Haworth co-indexing entry note]: "The Case for Non-Intrusive Research: A Virtual Reference Librarian's Perspective." Jensen, Bruce. Co-published simultaneously in *The Reference Librarian* (The Haworth Information Press, an imprint of The Haworth Press, Inc.) No. 85, 2004, pp. 139-149; and: *Digital versus Non-Digital Reference: Ask a Librarian Online and Offline* (ed: Jessamyn West) The Haworth Information Press, an imprint of The Haworth Press, Inc., 2004, pp. 139-149. Single or multiple copies of this article are available for a fee from The Haworth Document Delivery Service [1-800-HAWORTH, 9:00 a.m. - 5:00 p.m. (EST). E-mail address: docdelivery@haworthpress.com].

Digital Object Identifer: 10.1300/J120v41n85_11

INTRODUCTION

The other day a call came to me through the web portal of a major university that participates in our cooperative reference project. "I want literary criticism on Rilke," the questioner told me via Internet chat. "Where should I look?"

The question triggered fond memories of being an undergraduate, discovering Rilke, longing to know more about him and his poetry. "Are you familiar with the databases offered by your school's library?" I asked, looking forward to a fun reference interview. Then came the next chat message.

"No I am not. I want full-text." *This* brought me back down to earth. The discourse was unnatural: not many young chatsters bother to type out *No I am not* when the first two keystrokes alone will suffice. And the sentence that followed was a borderline non sequitur adorned with a bit of librarian jargon. Taking advantage of a pause in the other sessions I had going–online librarians spend *eons* waiting for chat responses–I googled the Rilke patron's e-mail address. Sure enough: she was a senior reference librarian at the university's library. Like Rilke himself in "The Poet," I felt suddenly uninspired. *O hour of my muse: why do you leave me/Wounding me by the wingbeats of your flight? Alone: what shall I use my mouth to utter?*[1] I wondered what I could possibly write to the soulless imposter on the other side of my computer screen.

The other patrons were showing signs of life and I did not care to indulge my ersatz undergraduate, the one I once dreamed of taking under my librarianly wing, *Martin Eden*-style. So the keys clicked bitterly, archly, as I typed, "It's astonishing that you, a reference librarian, would not know those resources!" Her response, when it finally came, was abashed but scarcely apologetic. I, seething inside, pleasantly reassured her and lost no time in disconnecting.

I do not screen many callers that way. But after more than two years of performing real-time virtual reference (VR) as my primary job, I know very well that a good many of my visitors are working librarians, MLIS students, and library school faculty posing questions whose answers they already know or do not care about.

Is there any harm in that? There certainly is. With a few important exceptions, such an imposition on AskA librarians' time only does a disservice to colleagues and, more painfully, to genuine patrons.

ILL-CONSIDERED RESEARCH

Recently a library school student announced on a statewide listserv his intention to survey the quality of reference work by asking a single question of several librarians and recording their handling of the query. Mentioning that he might include online librarians in the sample, he asked if anyone has done what he proposed. I wrote in response,

> Online reference librarians get a lot of calls from library science students and educators, as well as from working librarians curious about this type of service.
>
> Many "insider" patrons identify themselves up front. Many others don't. Occasionally these blow their cover one way or another, sometimes unwittingly, and it's questionable what they could hope to do with data gathered from such a transaction.
>
> One wonders if lawyers are studied in the same way as reference librarians. A survey of ten attorneys, to record how each one treats a single legal problem, might be interesting. It would surely cost a fortune, though. But, hey–librarians answer questions for free and don't charge by the minute.
>
> Or do they?
>
> If you bring a test question to an online librarian–or an in-the-flesh librarian–at a busy moment, inevitably you are going to affect the services that other questioners receive. Further, if you ask a real stumper that can't be answered right away and is thus kicked upstairs for further research, a certain quantity of costly MLIS person-hours will be invested in your question.
>
> Leaving aside concerns about research on human subjects (depending on whether you want to publish your findings or rather satisfy your own curiosity), please be conscious of your impact when you do this survey. When you ask for service at a reference desk, don't you normally tip your professional hat so the person serving you knows s/he can draw from a shared vocabulary and body of knowledge? Further, if your question is not such an urgent one, don't you normally make your visit to the desk at a slow moment?
>
> There's been a great deal of research on virtual reference transactions; they lend themselves to valuable analysis that would be impractical in other reference contexts. Anyone wanting to devise a truly novel survey would need to explore what's been done already . . . it's worth looking into ways that you might be able to ac-

cess a rich body of existing data, without having to pose as someone you're not.[2]

One would expect research on virtual reference to be a growth industry in academe: interest in VR is expanding, and detailed data are enticingly easy to gather. Whether such studies will be designed to minimize interference with the services under scrutiny, and whether they will generate legitimate findings, are the concerns of this paper.

UNOBTRUSIVE SURVEYS
AND UNWITTING OBSERVER ERROR

Well-organized reference staffs stay abreast of recurring questions as one means of increasing efficiency and enhancing services. Online reference teams similarly alert one another to likely queries, using e-mail or instant messaging to collaborate on good answers and to help co-workers identify relevant electronic resources. Typically such communication is prompted by current events or by a school assignment, such as a high school teacher urging students to use the Internet to gather information about sweatshop labor.

Occasionally warnings concerning another sort of assignment circulate among online librarians. The cooperative I work for has served as an ostensibly unknowing test subject for at least one library school professor who apparently instructed his students to stump us, and told them how to do so. A lead staff member lost no time in sending us e-mail alerts, noting that particular suspicious-sounding questions had been asked repeatedly by several different patrons; these alerts passed along resources to help us quickly and accurately respond to the questions. It is in our interest to be careful. Shortly after I was hired a work mate told me about a university instructor who had selected the worst reference interview transcripts gathered from such a project, with the intention of publishing the damning evidence and presenting it at library conferences. Nice work if you can get it.

Even without malicious intent or the use of repeated items, research using dummy question sets has obvious shortcomings. The chat discourse of an information professional or trainee presenting a sham query is very likely to differ from that of a genuine questioner; I have served patrons whose manner seemed to ooze falsity, and I cannot doubt this affected the level of service I provided.

Unobtrusive surveys, in which trained questioners impersonate genuine library users, have been used effectively by Childers and others to assess reference service in traditional settings.[3] The technique has been applied to synchronous digital reference by White, Abels, and Kaske;[4] their pilot study, while undoubtedly well designed, carefully conducted, and likely to be emulated by many, exemplifies a counterproductive approach dissonant with the nature of the new medium that it examines.

White et al. formulated a pool of 50 questions, trained a team of questioners, and used them to engage in online reference interviews. The precedents for this experimental design were established in studies of reference desk service, where such research strategies make perfect sense. Short of installing hidden cameras and having actual patrons wear a wire, unobtrusive surveys using sham questioners are the only way to closely observe the performance of desk librarians working under authentic conditions. The inherent imperfections of this design—that the questions and the questioners are at best only good imitations of the real thing, and that the study itself consumes library resources which could be spent instead on real patrons—is the price that must be paid for an intimate view of the reference desk from the user's side.

Studies like that of White et al. sustain these imperfections, but in a realm where they are entirely unwarranted. Given that thousands of genuine questions pour in to busy online reference services every month, it is absurd to fuss over the creation of fifty questions that *seem* authentic. And while the perspective of a trained participant-observer is essential in obtaining a reasonably faithful account of reference desk transactions, electronic reference interviews are recorded, word for misspelled word, and preserved in transcripts.

Time spent by investigators on devising questions and training people in how to ask them would be better used in developing descriptive taxonomies of actual question types and in analyzing transcripts. Their existence in electronic form facilitates the use of corpus analysis—used by linguists such as Douglas Biber and Michael Stubbs to shed astonishing new light on language use[5]—along with other analytical techniques previously beyond the reach of library science research. A robust, detailed, and research-ready body of data is being generated 24 hours a day without the intervention of investigators.

This discussion of reference interview transcripts as a window into VR ought to raise serious questions about threats to the privacy of patrons and librarians. In fact, the removal of names and other identifiers, which is necessary before releasing transcripts to researchers, is not routinely performed by many online reference services. As things stand currently, a government agency exerting its powers under the USA

PATRIOT Act would be able to mine raw transcript files for significant amounts of potentially sensitive data. Systematically stripping transcripts of personal information is something that *should* be done regularly; VR providers would thus be protecting users and librarians while simultaneously preparing usable data for study.

WHY A LIBRARIAN WOULD ASK A LIBRARIAN

There are a number of reasons, of varying degrees of legitimacy, that library professionals put themselves in the position of VR patrons. They do so in order to:

- Inform management decisions between competing service providers
- Analyze interfaces
- Observe librarian discourse and behavior
- Observe patron behavior
- Demonstrate VR for webliographic instruction and other teaching purposes
- Train, and monitor the performance of, online librarians under their supervision
- Satisfy idle curiosity.

Decisions between VR providers. Faced with choosing among virtual reference services in competition for a contract, library managers would be unwise to rely on vendors' assessments of the quality of their own services. Requesting to view representative transcripts is worthwhile, but allows the vendor to selectively skew the sample. Should it be impractical to arrange trial periods with each provider, during which patron satisfaction could be closely monitored, it would make perfect sense for the library to surreptitiously direct questions toward each of the services under consideration and to evaluate the responses.

One sensible way to do this is to engage in-house reference staff in a systematic appraisal. Without identifying themselves, staffers could pass along to the competing services questions not readily answerable at the desk, keeping logs of the quality and promptness of the responses. A test done this way would not force colleagues to waste time on bogus questions. The results could contribute to an informed assessment of the strengths and weaknesses of each service.

Analysis of interfaces. Judging ease of use of the patron-side interface is important in selection, design, and ongoing redesign. But such assessment never requires that a librarian masquerade as a user. Hands-on work with the VR interface should be arranged through system managers to take place in a practice or training queue to avoid interference with patrons and librarians engaged in actual transactions.

Empirical research on librarian performance. Using canned questions and trained questioners for this purpose leads to results that are less than accurate. What is more, it is an irresponsible misuse of the time of librarians and research assistants. The characteristics of chat reference provide researchers and AskA services a historic opportunity to revolutionize how reference is studied. Electronic transcripts of online sessions comprise a formidable mine of data–easily tens of thousands of transactions, untainted by the presence of an observer–that could yield important findings in the hands of imaginative investigators. Text analysis using powerful tools of corpus linguistics could shed new kinds of light on both sides of the virtual reference desk.

Proprietors of these transcripts must find ways to make their data widely available in cooperation with responsible researchers. A tiny example of what is at stake can be seen in the extensive log of e-mail reference questions received between 1997 and 2001 by one New Jersey library and posted voluntarily on the Web by Sarah Weissman.[6]

Research on patrons. It is notable and inexplicable that user satisfaction with digital reference remains underanalyzed. Janes, in his survey of more than 600 electronic reference librarians, found that less than ten percent had tried to systematically examine the feelings of users toward their services.[7]

The facile strategy of inviting patrons to complete an online questionnaire at the conclusion of their VR sessions, like too many other library user surveys, nets an exceptional, self-selected sample. In my experience, some few users do spend the extra time on end-of-session questionnaires, but the majority close the window and move on. In fact many patrons disconnect the reference interview itself unceremoniously, even mysteriously, the moment they feel their information needs have been met, or thwarted, or the moment their browsers crash. One almost never knows, in the moment, why they vanish.

Though affective measures are not easily operationalized, online reference transcripts simplify quantitative measurement of user behavior. Sloan[8] shows what is possible for anyone with access to a database of reference transcripts; studies like these illustrate how readily one can run elaborate breakdowns of duration of calls, number of calls per day throughout a year or semester, wait times, types of questions received and what times of day they arrive, and many other quantifiable variables relevant to user response.

Demonstration. Librarians and educators would do well to familiarize patrons and students with electronic reference services. Ours has had visitors who identify themselves up front as university professors in the middle of lecturing a class, or as librarians introducing co-workers to VR. In this type of bibliographic instruction, a brick-and-mortar library analogy is useful: no teacher should expect a desk librarian to properly accommodate a visiting class that had not bothered to schedule the visit. Astonishingly, I have experienced several incidents when patron traffic suddenly surged and all the questions were similar–this happens when a schoolteacher brings a class to a computer lab and instructs the pupils to use us to find an answer. A dozen calls directed at one or two librarians can effectively paralyze the service and thus do nothing to help students understand the benefits of using VR; quite the contrary.

Training. Supervisors of online reference librarians might choose to probe staff members' skills by logging in anonymously to pose particular types of questions. While this can quickly identify problem areas where more training or practice is desirable, caution should be exercised: done carelessly or excessively, such an intrusion can engender ill will among employees who might not be fooled by the questioner's aliases. Here too, transcripts reveal strengths and weaknesses that merit attention; they furnish insights into the crew that can help focus and streamline the staff development process. Ward's recent article suggests means of using transcript to help improve performance.[9]

Idle curiosity. Given the novelty of synchronous virtual reference, it is unsurprisingly common to see colleagues' calls of this nature. Ideally the questioner presents the intention of the visit and his or her identity– "I'm a librarian in Smallville and I'm just curious to see how this online reference thing works"–at the opening of the transaction. Such an introduction is the best way to get a real cook's tour; the librarian picking up the call will ordinarily be pleased to demonstrate the software's features and respond expansively to questions about her work, if time permits. If it does not, she will likely suggest a more propitious time of day for such a visit. When professional visitors identify themselves, they tacitly grant the librarian the option of terminating the session if it happens to be interfering with calls from genuine patrons.

A librarian might choose, for some private reason, to approach the service in disguise. The ethical ice here is dangerously thin. There can be no argument that posing a question whose answer is already known by, or does not matter to, the questioner is an abuse of resources.

HOW INTRUSIONS DEGRADE VR SERVICE

The profound impact of extraneous calls on live electronic reference service would be difficult to overstate. The faceless virtual librarian has a mere tenuous hold on patron attention and loyalty, and a questioner who becomes impatient is apt to disconnect quickly. The time required to locate and push pages, as well as to merely respond to chat messages, varies significantly according to the number of patrons being served at a given moment. There are various reasons for this, some of them software-related.

At the librarian interface used in our service, for example, it is simple enough to establish concurrent connections with multiple patrons, but impossible to simultaneously carry on communication with more than one at a time. Moving from one caller to another does not happen instantly, as with a telephone switchboard; rather, the VR console can take several seconds to reload when we choose to address a patron other than the currently "active" questioner. When working with a single patron we have the luxury of an uninterrupted connection, but as soon as another is added, the librarian begins to do what we call "juggling." This metaphor is apt–what happens at a busy reference desk is fundamentally different because waiting patrons are aware of one another and are normally bound by conventions of turn-taking behavior. In the electronic setting, attention devoted to any particular questioner must of course be reduced markedly as their numbers increase, but patrons log on in isolation to AskA services. Thus they may be unlikely to understand or accept that they are not receiving the undivided attention of a librarian, and they may be impatient with delays in responses. Hence, just as a juggler who adds one ball after another soon reaches a point when balls start to drop, even a practiced librarian serving multiple patrons will lose users due to unavoidable compromises to the speed as well as the quality of the service s/he can offer.

Clandestine questioning is disruptive in real time, but its drain on the VR resource does not end when the false questioner disconnects. Our service offers follow-up and second-level reference services for those whose questions cannot be answered satisfactorily during the initial interview. These questions are routed to local libraries, to subject specialists in such fields as law, medicine, art, and business, and to librarians with a variety of language skills. The answers are generally thorough because plenty of expensive MLIS time is spent on reaching them, yet sometimes the effort is in vain: some replies bounce when sent to phony e-mail addresses, and it is impossible to know how many others are requested by counterfeit patrons with no real need for the answers.

CONCLUSION

There will always be researchers convinced that their own work somehow trumps the work and lives of the people under study. Even Whitlatch endorses unobtrusive research in virtual reference in an otherwise excellent article–in which, with unintentional irony, she notes that truly ethical research must first of all avoid harming the participants.[10] Effective investigators, while not losing sight of aims cogently spelled out by the likes of Whitlatch, Novotny,[11] and others with a compelling concern for improving the quality of reference services, must take a hard, fresh look at their methods. They should be willing to recognize that applying convenient but unsuitable techniques to VR diminishes the quality of their findings and damages library services.

It would be healthy for the Information Studies academic community to remember the accomplishments of Elfreda Chatman and others who have applied participatory action research to questions in our field. IS scholars too often ignore–at librarianship's peril–essential tenets of this research ethic, with its crucial principle of sharing findings with those being studied. Study subjects who realize no benefits from their participation come to resent being treated as mere implements. Conversely, Garner's account[12] of the successful use of action research to improve reference service delivery at an Australian library presents a model worthy of emulation.

Reference research, if it is to be useful and humane, must begin from the intention of openly informing, and not clandestinely deceiving, members of the growing VR workforce. Surely this ideal of action research is consistent with librarians' capacity to interpret and use information. Those of us who care about our work welcome scrutiny that leads to helpful feedback and more effective service. Researchers should never lose sight of the fact that their work is at best a means to this noble end.

Managers of virtual reference services are able to marshal vast pools of useful data, generated by fascinating interactions with authentic patrons. Investigators should learn to take full advantage of the possibilities offered by warehoused transcript databases–and in the interest of better reference service, managers should look for ways to accommodate requests from the academic community. Such cooperation will save a lot of frankly wasted time and expense, and will lead to exciting advances in our understanding of the reference transaction.

ENDNOTES

1. Rilke, Rainer Maria (1985), *Rainer Maria Rilke: Selected Poems.* Trans. Albert Ernest Flemming. Methuen: New York.

2. Jensen, Bruce. "Re: Query." California Library Association Listserv. <calix@listproc.sjsu.edu> 4-18-2003.

3. See for example Childers, Thomas, "The Test of Reference," *Library Journal* 105 (1980): 924-928.

4. White, Marilyn Domas, Eileen G. Abels, and Neal Kaske, "Evaluation of Chat Reference Service Quality: Pilot Study," *D-Lib Magazine* 9, no. 2 (Feb 2003). Online, <http://www.dlib.org/dlib/february03/white/02white.html>. Accessed: 5-6-2003.

5. See for example Biber, Douglas, Susan Conrad, and Randi Reppen (1998), *Corpus Linguistics: Investigating Language Structure and Use*, Cambridge University Press: New York; and Stubbs, Michael (1996), *Text and Corpus Analysis: Computer-Assisted Studies of Language and Culture (Language in Society*, 23), Blackwell Publishers: Cambridge, MA.

6. Weissman, Sarah, *Electronic Reference at Morris County Library.* Online, <http://www.gti.net/mocolib1/mclweb/eref.html>. Accessed: 5-6-2003.

7. Janes, Joseph, "Digital Reference: Reference Libraries' Experiences and Attitudes," *Journal of the American Society for Information Science and Technology* 53, no. 7 (May 2002): 549-566.

8. Sloan, Bernie. *Ready for Reference: Academic Libraries Offer Live Web-Based Reference. Evaluating System Use* (July 11, 2001). Online, <http://www.lis.uiuc.edu/~b-sloan/r4r.final.htm>. Accessed: 5-5-2003.

9. Ward, David, "Using virtual reference transcripts for staff training," *Reference Services Review* 31, no. 1 (2003); 46-56.

10. Jo Bell Whitlatch, "Evaluating Reference Services in the Electronic Age," *Library Trends* 50 (Fall 2001): 207-217.

11. Novotny, Eric, "Evaluating Electronic Reference Services: Issues, Approaches and Criteria," *The Reference Librarian* 74 (2001): 103-120.

12. Garner, Imogen, "New Reference: Diversifying Service Delivery," presented at the 1999 Conference of the International Association of Technological University Libraries (IATUL), Chania, Greece 17th May-21st May, 1999. Online, <http://educate.lib.chalmers.se/IATUL/proceedcontents/chanpap/garner.html>. Accessed: 5-7-2003.

Index

BOOK ORDER FORM!

Order a copy of this book with this form or online at:
http://www.haworthpress.com/store/product.asp?sku=5162

Digital versus Non-Digital Reference
Ask a Librarian Online and Offline

_____ in softbound at $29.95 (ISBN: 0-7890-2443-8)
_____ in hardbound at $49.95 (ISBN: 0-7890-2442-X)

COST OF BOOKS _____

POSTAGE & HANDLING _____
US: $4.00 for first book & $1.50
for each additional book
Outside US: $5.00 for first book
& $2.00 for each additional book.

SUBTOTAL _____

In Canada: add 7% GST. _____

STATE TAX _____
CA, IL, IN, MN, NY, OH & SD residents
please add appropriate local sales tax.

FINAL TOTAL _____
If paying in Canadian funds, convert
using the current exchange rate,
UNESCO coupons welcome.

❏ BILL ME LATER:
Bill-me option is good on US/Canada/
Mexico orders only; not good to jobbers,
wholesalers, or subscription agencies.

❏ Signature _____

❏ Payment Enclosed: $ _____

❏ PLEASE CHARGE TO MY CREDIT CARD:
❏ Visa ❏ MasterCard ❏ AmEx ❏ Discover
❏ Diner's Club ❏ Eurocard ❏ JCB

Account # _____

Exp Date _____

Signature _____
(Prices in US dollars and subject to change without notice.)

PLEASE PRINT ALL INFORMATION OR ATTACH YOUR BUSINESS CARD

Name

Address

City   State/Province   Zip/Postal Code

Country

Tel   Fax

E-Mail

May we use your e-mail address for confirmations and other types of information? ❏ Yes ❏ No We appreciate receiving
your e-mail address. Haworth would like to e-mail special discount offers to you, as a preferred customer.
We will never share, rent, or exchange your e-mail address. We regard such actions as an invasion of your privacy.

Order From Your **Local Bookstore** or Directly From
The Haworth Press, Inc. 10 Alice Street, Binghamton, New York 13904-1580 • USA
Call Our toll-free number (1-800-429-6784) / Outside US/Canada: (607) 722-5857
Fax: 1-800-895-0582 / Outside US/Canada: (607) 771-0012
E-mail your order to us: orders@haworthpress.com

For orders outside US and Canada, you may wish to order through your local
sales representative, distributor, or bookseller.
For information, see http://haworthpress.com/distributors

(Discounts are available for individual orders in US and Canada only, not booksellers/distributors.)

Please photocopy this form for your personal use.
www.HaworthPress.com

BOF04